MW00635790

the Entertaining COOKBOOK

the Entertaining COOKBOOK

SOUTHERN LADY'S BEST TABLES, RECIPES & PARTY MENUS

VOLUME 2

hm | books

hm | books

PRESIDENT/CCO Brian Hart Hoffman
VICE PRESIDENT/EDITORIAL Cindy Smith Cooper
ART DIRECTOR Karissa Brown

SOUTHERN LADY EDITORIAL

EDITOR Kathleen Johnston Whaley
ART DIRECTOR Tracy Wood-Franklin
MANAGING EDITOR Lisa Frederick
EDITORIAL COORDINATOR Becky Goff
ASSOCIATE EDITOR Mona Moore
ASSISTANT EDITOR Elizabeth Bonner
RECIPE EDITOR Fran Jensen
COPY EDITOR Nancy Ogburn
EDITORIAL CONTRIBUTORS Karen Callaway,
Lauren Eberle, Andrea Fanning, K. Faith Morgan
STYLIST Tracey MacMillan Runnion
CONTRIBUTING STYLISTS Beverly Farrington,
Amanda Bailey Leach, Katherine Tucker,
Adrienne A. Williams
SENIOR PHOTOGRAPHERS Marcy Black Simpson,
John O'Hagan
PHOTOGRAPHERS Jim Bathie, William Dickey,
Stephanie Welbourne
ASSISTANT PHOTOGRAPHER Caroline Smith
CONTRIBUTING PHOTOGRAPHER Stephen DeVries
FOOD STYLISTS/RECIPE DEVELOPERS
Mary-Claire Britton, Melissa Gray, Kathleen Kanen,
Janet Lambert, Vanessa Rocchio, Loren Wood
CONTRIBUTING FOOD STYLISTS/RECIPE DEVELOPERS
Jane Drennen, Virginia Hornbuckle, Anna Theoktisto
TEST KITCHEN ASSISTANT Anita Simpson Spain
SENIOR DIGITAL IMAGING SPECIALIST
Delisa McDaniel
DIGITAL IMAGING SPECIALIST Clark Densmore

hm
hoffmanmedia

CHAIRMAN OF THE BOARD/CEO Phyllis Hoffman DePiano
PRESIDENT/COO Eric W. Hoffman
PRESIDENT/CCO Brian Hart Hoffman
EXECUTIVE VICE PRESIDENT/CFO Mary P. Cummings
EXECUTIVE VICE PRESIDENT/ OPERATIONS & MANUFACTURING
Greg Baugh
VICE PRESIDENT/DIGITAL MEDIA Jon Adamson
VICE PRESIDENT/EDITORIAL Cindy Smith Cooper
VICE PRESIDENT/ADMINISTRATION Lynn Lee Terry

Copyright © 2016 by Hoffman Media
Publishers of *Southern Lady* magazine

All rights reserved. No part of this book may be reproduced
or transmitted in any form or by any means, electronic or
mechanical, including photocopying, or by any information
storage and retrieval system, without permission in writing from
Hoffman Media. Reviewers may quote brief passages for specific
inclusion in a magazine or newspaper.

Hoffman Media
1900 International Park Drive, Suite 50
Birmingham, Alabama 35243
www.hoffmanmedia.com

ISBN # 978-1-940772-30-1

Printed in China

On the cover: Take the festivities outdoors where the garden
lends a natural complement to a flower-filled setting.

Introduction

To have company or to entertain in the South is a lovely way to open our homes and share hospitality and warm conversation. Of course, most of our gatherings would not be complete without food, and serving a lineup of delicious dishes is frequently the focus of Southern hostesses preparing for company. Oftentimes heirloom tableware and linens compose an inviting setting, and perhaps a well-tended garden provides flowers and greenery for a freshly clipped centerpiece.

We at *Southern Lady* have assembled this entertaining volume and cookbook for convenience so that you can refer to it over and over again. Inside you'll find a variety of menus and a section of additional recipes to help in planning occasions grand and small, formal and casual. The compilation keeps these editor- and reader-favorites in one handy place so that you can reference recipes seen in previous issues rather than keep up with cards or copies you might have made in the past. The selection includes everyday classics, as well as seasonal menus to entertain friends and family throughout the year.

To loyal *Southern Lady* magazine readers and to hostesses at heart who love to receive guests, we are delighted to present Volume 2 of *The Entertaining Cookbook*. We hope it helps create many happy memories!

ENTERTAINING COOKBOOK

VOL. 2

Dining
AT HOME

*Pretty table settings, a beautiful
flower arrangement, and flavorful,
homemade dishes add joy
to any occasion shared at home.*

Lovely Night

Play the part of your own fairy godmother, and transform an ordinary dinner
into an unforgettable evening with your Prince Charming.

Caesar Salad for Two

Makes 2 to 4 servings

- ½ (8.5-ounce) French baguette, cut into 1-inch cubes
- ¼ cup butter, melted
- ¼ teaspoon garlic powder
- ¼ teaspoon seasoned salt
- ¼ teaspoon ground black pepper
- 1 heart of romaine lettuce, chopped

Shaved Parmesan cheese
Caesar Dressing (recipe follows)

1. Preheat oven to 400°. Line a rimmed baking sheet with foil.

2. In a medium bowl, combine bread cubes, melted butter, garlic powder, seasoned salt, and pepper. Spread bread cubes in an even layer on prepared pan. Bake for 10 minutes or until browned and crispy.

3. In a medium bowl, combine lettuce, cheese, and croutons; toss gently. Drizzle with Caesar Dressing right before serving.

CAESAR DRESSING

Makes about 1 cup

- ⅓ cup mayonnaise
- ¼ cup water
- 1 tablespoon Dijon mustard
- 1 tablespoon Champagne vinegar
- 1 tablespoon fresh lemon juice
- ½ teaspoon garlic powder
- ¼ teaspoon salt
- ¼ teaspoon ground black pepper
- ½ cup extra-light olive oil

1. In the container of a blender, combine mayonnaise, water, Dijon, vinegar, lemon juice, garlic powder, salt, and pepper. Process until well blended. With blender running, drizzle in olive oil in a slow, steady stream. Cover, and refrigerate until ready to serve. Store in an airtight container for up to 2 weeks.

Glass Slipper

Makes 4 servings

- ½ cup water
- ¼ cup sugar
- 1 cup almond liqueur
- 2 tablespoons fresh lemon juice
- 2 tablespoons fresh lime juice
- 1 (750-milliliter) bottle Champagne, chilled

Garnish: lemon slices, lime slices, fresh mint sprigs

1. In a small saucepan, combine water and sugar over medium-high heat, stirring until sugar dissolves. Remove from heat, and let cool completely.

2. In a small pitcher, combine sugar mixture, almond liqueur, lemon juice, and lime juice, stirring well. Add Champagne, stirring gently to combine. Garnish with lemon slices, lime slices, and fresh mint sprigs, if desired.

menu

Glass Slipper
Caesar Salad for Two
Roasted Kale
Shrimp Scampi and Linguini
Hazelnut Mousse

Roasted Kale
Makes 2 to 4 servings

1 bunch kale, chopped
1 shallot, thinly sliced
¼ cup teriyaki sauce
2 tablespoons olive oil
¼ teaspoon ground black pepper

1. Preheat oven to 375°. Line a rimmed baking sheet with foil.

2. In a medium bowl, combine kale, shallot, teriyaki sauce, olive oil, and pepper, tossing to coat. Spread kale mixture in an even layer on prepared pan. Bake for 10 minutes.

Shrimp Scampi and Linguini
Makes 2 to 4 servings

8 ounces linguini noodles
1½ pounds large fresh shrimp, peeled and deveined (tails on)
1½ teaspoons seasoned salt
2 tablespoons olive oil
¼ cup plus ½ cup cold butter, divided
1 (8-ounce) container sliced baby portobello mushrooms
1 red bell pepper, chopped
1 cup chopped green onion
2 tablespoons minced garlic
¾ teaspoon salt
½ teaspoon ground black pepper
½ cup white wine
Garnish: chopped fresh parsley

1. Cook pasta according to package directions; set aside.

2. In a medium bowl, combine shrimp and seasoned salt, tossing to coat.

3. In a large nonstick skillet, heat olive oil over medium-high heat. Cook shrimp, in batches, for 1 minute per side, until lightly browned. Set aside.

4. In skillet, melt ¼ cup butter over medium heat. Add mushrooms, bell pepper, green onion, garlic, salt, and pepper; cook for 8 minutes, stirring occasionally. Add wine; cook for 2 minutes. Gradually add remaining ½ cup butter, in pieces, whisking to combine well. Add shrimp; cook for 1 minute, until heated through. Serve shrimp mixture over pasta. Garnish with parsley, if desired.

DINNER AT HOME

16

Hazelnut Mousse

Makes 2 to 4 servings

- 1 cup heavy whipping cream, divided
- ½ cup chocolate-hazelnut spread
- Garnish: fresh strawberries, confectioners' sugar

1. In a medium bowl, combine ¼ cup cream and chocolate-hazelnut spread. Beat with a mixer at medium-high speed until creamy. Add remaining ¾ cup cream, beating until stiff peaks form. Garnish with fresh strawberries and confectioners' sugar, if desired.

Table for Two

Celebrate a special anniversary
or treasured sisterhood with a delicious
meal served alfresco.

Make dinnertime truly special with a table for two in sunset
hues. For a subtle nod to the season, choose a tablecloth with
a bold floral motif; china with an equally eye-catching pattern
adds to the presentation. An artful menu relies on garden-
fresh ingredients, and pink hydrangeas add that extra touch
of Southern charm.

menu

Honey-Orange Prosecco

Salmon with
Bourbon-Pecan Glaze

Rosemary-Scented Couscous

Roasted Asparagus
with Orange Butter

Lemon Custard

Honey-Orange Prosecco

Makes 2 servings

3 tablespoons honey
3 tablespoons lime juice
¼ cup orange liqueur, chilled
1½ cups Prosecco, chilled
Garnish: honeysuckle

1. In a large pitcher, combine honey and lime juice until honey dissolves. Stir in liqueur. Slowly add Prosecco, stirring gently to combine. Pour into champagne flutes. Garnish with honeysuckle, if desired.

Salmon with Bourbon-Pecan Glaze

Makes 2 servings

¼ teaspoon salt
¼ teaspoon ground black pepper
2 (6-ounce) skinless salmon fillets
1 tablespoon olive oil
2 tablespoons butter, divided
2 tablespoons bourbon
½ cup brown sugar
½ cup finely chopped pecans

1. Preheat oven to 425°.

2. Sprinkle salt and pepper evenly over salmon.

3. In a large oven-safe pan, heat olive oil and 1 tablespoon butter over medium-high heat until melted. Add salmon, and cook for 1 to 2 minutes or until browned. Turn fish over. Cook for 1 to 2 minutes.

4. In a small saucepan, combine bourbon and brown sugar, and bring to a boil over

medium-high heat. Boil for 2 to 3 minutes or until sugar dissolves. Stir in pecans and remaining 1 tablespoon butter.

5. Spoon pecan mixture evenly over browned salmon fillets, and place pan in oven. Bake for 8 to 10 minutes or until fish flakes easily with a fork.

Rosemary-Scented Couscous

Makes 2 servings

1 cup chicken broth
¾ cup couscous
½ teaspoon lemon zest
¼ teaspoon minced fresh rosemary

1. In a medium saucepan, bring chicken broth to a boil over medium-high heat. Stir in couscous; cover, and let stand for 10 minutes. Fluff with fork. Stir in lemon zest and rosemary. Serve immediately.

Roasted Asparagus with Orange Butter

Makes 2 servings

½ pound asparagus
1 tablespoon olive oil
⅛ teaspoon salt
⅛ teaspoon ground black pepper
1 tablespoon softened butter
1 tablespoon orange zest
1 garlic clove, minced

1. Preheat oven to 425°. Line a baking sheet with foil.

2. Arrange asparagus in a single layer on prepared pan. Drizzle with olive oil; sprinkle with salt and pepper. Bake for 10 to 12 minutes or until asparagus is browned and tender.

3. In a large bowl, combine butter, orange zest, and garlic. Toss roasted asparagus in butter mixture.

"Summer afternoon, summer afternoon; to me those have always been the two most beautiful words in the English language."
—Henry James

Lemon Custard
Makes 2 servings

1   cup whole milk
½   cup whipping cream
1   tablespoon lemon zest
1   rosemary sprig
⅓   cup sugar
3   tablespoons cornstarch
¼   teaspoon salt
5   egg yolks
3   tablespoons lemon juice
½   tablespoon butter
    Garnish: Heart Shortbread Cookies
    (recipe follows)

1. In a medium saucepan, combine milk, cream, lemon zest, and rosemary. Using the back of a spoon, press rosemary lightly to release flavor. Heat over medium-high heat until tiny bubbles form around edge of pan. Strain into a bowl.

2. In a large saucepan, combine sugar, cornstarch, and salt. Gradually whisk in hot milk mixture. Heat over medium heat, whisking constantly, until thick. Remove from heat.

3. In a large bowl, whisk egg yolks. Add cornstarch mixture to egg yolks in a slow, steady stream, whisking constantly. Heat over medium heat until boiling. Stir in lemon juice and butter. Pour into individual bowls; cover, and refrigerate for at least 4 hours. Garnish with Heart Shortbread Cookies, if desired.

HEART SHORTBREAD COOKIES
Makes 8 cookies

½   cup all-purpose flour
2   tablespoons sugar, divided
½   teaspoon lemon zest
⅛   teaspoon salt
¼   cup butter, cut into small pieces

1. Preheat oven to 350°. Line a baking sheet with parchment paper.

2. In a large bowl, combine flour, 1 table-spoon sugar, lemon zest, and salt. Using a pastry blender, cut butter into flour mixture. Combine until a dough forms.

3. On a lightly floured surface, roll dough to a ¼-inch thickness. Using a 1-inch heart-shaped cutter, press into dough. Place hearts on prepared pan. Reroll scraps, if necessary. Sprinkle with remaining 1 tablespoon sugar. Bake for 8 to 10 minutes or until lightly browned. Let cool on pan for 2 minutes. Transfer to a wire rack, and let cool completely. Store in an airtight container.

A Charleston Brunch

Join us in a celebration of Southern graces and signature flavors at Charleston's enchanting Two Meeting Street Inn, where live oaks, fragrant blossoms, and Battery breezes set the scene for an extraordinary morning meal.

menu

Two Meeting Street

Fresh Fruit in Vanilla-Bean-
and-Cardamom Syrup

Sausage Cornmeal
Casserole with Fiesta Salsa

Praline French Toast

Two Meeting Street
Makes 4 to 6 servings

- 1 cup pineapple juice, chilled
- 1 cup orange juice, chilled
- 2 tablespoons grenadine
- 1 tablespoon fresh lemon juice
- 1 cup Prosecco, chilled
- ½ ounce orange liqueur

1. In a small pitcher, combine pineapple juice, orange juice, grenadine, and lemon juice, stirring to combine. Add Prosecco and orange liqueur, stirring gently to combine.

Fresh Fruit in Vanilla-Bean-and-Cardamom Syrup
Makes 4 servings

- 1 cup water
- 1 cup sugar
- 1 vanilla bean, split and scraped, seeds reserved
- ½ teaspoon ground cardamom
- 1 cup fresh raspberries
- 1 cup fresh blueberries
- 1 cup sliced fresh strawberries
- 1 large orange, sectioned
- 2 tablespoons fresh lime juice

1. In a small saucepan, combine water and sugar over medium-high heat; stir until sugar dissolves. Add vanilla bean, vanilla bean seeds, and cardamom, whisking to combine well. Reduce heat to medium, and cook for 5 minutes. Remove and discard vanilla bean. Let cool completely.

2. In a small bowl, combine syrup mixture, raspberries, blueberries, strawberries, orange sections, and lime juice, stirring to combine well. Cover, and refrigerate for at least 1 hour.

1 (7-ounce) can whole-kernel yellow corn with red and green bell peppers, drained
2 tablespoons chopped fresh parsley
½ teaspoon ground cumin
½ teaspoon garlic powder
½ teaspoon salt

1. In a medium bowl, combine black beans, tomatoes, corn, parsley, cumin, garlic powder, and salt, stirring to combine. Cover, and refrigerate until ready to serve.

Praline French Toast
Makes 2 servings

½ cup heavy whipping cream
1 large egg
1 tablespoon sugar
¼ teaspoon ground cinnamon
¼ teaspoon ground nutmeg
1 teaspoon vanilla extract
2 tablespoons butter
2 English muffins, split
Praline Sauce (recipe follows)
Garnish: chopped toasted pecans

1. In a small bowl, whisk together cream, egg, sugar, cinnamon, nutmeg, and vanilla.

2. In a medium nonstick skillet, heat butter over medium heat until melted.

3. Dip English muffins into cream mixture, allowing excess to drain. Cook for 3 to 4 minutes per side or until golden brown. Serve with Praline Sauce. Garnish with pecans, if desired.

PRALINE SAUCE
Makes 2 servings

¼ cup butter
1/3 cup firmly packed light brown sugar
1 tablespoon light corn syrup
1 tablespoon water

1. In a small saucepan, heat butter over medium heat until melted. Add brown sugar, corn syrup, and water; cook for 3 to 4 minutes, stirring constantly.

Sausage Cornmeal Casserole with Fiesta Salsa
Makes 2 servings

1½ cups shredded Cheddar cheese
1 cup finely chopped smoked sausage
1 (14.5-ounce) can fire-roasted diced tomatoes, well drained
¾ cup buttermilk self-rising cornmeal mix
1 (8-ounce) can cream-style corn
½ cup whole milk
¼ cup melted butter
1 large egg
½ teaspoon garlic powder
Fiesta Salsa (recipe follows)

1. Preheat oven to 400°. Spray 2 (12-ounce) baking dishes with cooking spray.

2. In a small bowl, combine cheese, sausage, and tomatoes.

3. In a separate bowl, combine cornmeal mix, corn, milk, butter, egg, and garlic powder, stirring to combine well. Layer half of cornmeal mixture into bottoms of prepared dishes. Divide cheese/sausage mixture between dishes, and layer over cornmeal mixture. Top with remaining cornmeal mixture. Bake for 25 to 30 minutes or until golden brown. Serve with Fiesta Salsa.

FIESTA SALSA
Makes 6 to 8 servings

1 (15-ounce) can black beans, rinsed and drained
1 (10-ounce) can tomatoes with green chiles, undrained

Putting on the Ritz

Invite your favorite flappers and flyboys to a meal that celebrates the very best of the era that introduced the world to jazz, jive, and Jay Gatsby.

Don your glad rags, and put on your swanky jewels for a party that's pos-i-lute-ly the cat's meow. The rich and royal hues of this setting leave no doubt that this is a grand gathering, so polish the silver, and light the tapers to bring the proper sparkle to the table. Add layers of luxurious linens and beautiful floral arrangements to heighten the allure and step up the glamour on this special night. And to be certain the evening hits on all sixes, serve a dinner with a menu that's truly the bee's knees.

menu

The Charleston

The Flapper

West Egg Strip Steaks
with Lobster Newburg Sauce

Roaring Twenties
Roasted Caesar Salad

Classic Roasted Red Potatoes

Speakeasy Shrimp with Lindy
Hoppin' John Cocktail Relish

Jazz Age Bread Pudding

The Charleston

Makes about 2 quarts

  4 cups pineapple juice, chilled
  4 cups orange juice, chilled
  1 cup vodka
  ¼ cup grenadine
  1 (750-milliliter) bottle Champagne,
     chilled
  Garnish: orange curls

1. In a large pitcher, combine pineapple juice, orange juice, vodka, and grenadine, stirring to combine.

2. To serve, add Champagne, stirring gently to combine. Garnish with orange curls, if desired.

The Flapper

Makes 1 drink

  2½ ounces gin
  ¼ ounce dry vermouth
  ¼ ounce fresh lime juice
  Garnish: lime slices

1. Fill a shaker halfway with ice cubes. Add gin, vermouth, and lime juice to shaker. Shake mixture vigorously for 5 to 10 seconds. Strain into a chilled cocktail glass. Garnish with lime slices, if desired.

West Egg Strip Steaks with Lobster Newburg Sauce

Makes 8 servings

  2 tablespoons garlic powder
  2 tablespoons onion powder
  1 tablespoon salt
  1½ teaspoons ground black pepper
  8 (8-ounce) New York strip steaks
     (about 1 inch thick)
  ¼ cup plus 2 tablespoons olive oil,
     divided
  Lobster Newburg Sauce (recipe follows)
  Garnish: chopped fresh parsley

1. Preheat oven to 400°. Line a large rimmed baking sheet with foil; set aside.

2. In a small bowl, combine garlic powder, onion powder, salt, and pepper.

3. Rub both sides of steaks with ¼ cup olive oil. Evenly sprinkle garlic powder mixture on both sides of steaks.

4. In a large nonstick skillet, heat remaining 2 tablespoons olive oil over medium-high heat. Cook steaks, in batches, for 2 to 3 minutes per side or until well browned. Place on prepared pan.

5. Prepare Lobster Newburg Sauce, and keep warm.

6. To finish, place steaks in oven for 4 to 5 minutes or until desired degree of doneness is reached. Top steaks with Lobster Newburg Sauce. Garnish with parsley, if desired.

Note: As an optional garnish, purchase a few extra lobster tails, and sauté in butter. Add to top of cooked steak, and then cover with Lobster Newburg Sauce.

1. Preheat oven to 450°. Line a large rimmed baking sheet with foil.

2. Place romaine cut side up on prepared pan.

3. In a small bowl, combine olive oil, lemon juice, 1 teaspoon salt, garlic powder, and ½ teaspoon pepper, whisking to combine. Using a pastry brush, brush cut sides of romaine with olive oil mixture, coating evenly.

4. In a small bowl, combine panko, Parmesan cheese, parsley, remaining ½ teaspoon salt, and remaining ¼ teaspoon pepper. Add melted butter, stirring to combine well. Divide panko mixture evenly on tops of romaine hearts. Bake for 4 to 5 minutes or just until outer leaves begin to wilt. Serve immediately.

LOBSTER NEWBURG SAUCE
Makes 8 servings

- 6   tablespoons butter
- 3   tablespoons all-purpose flour
- 2   cups heavy whipping cream
- 3   egg yolks, lightly beaten
- 2   cups coarsely chopped uncooked lobster meat
- ¼   cup dry sherry
- 2   tablespoons lemon juice
- ½   teaspoon salt

1. In a large skillet, heat butter over medium heat until melted. Add flour; cook for 1 minute, whisking constantly. Gradually add cream, whisking until smooth. Cook for 3 to 4 minutes or until sauce begins to thicken.

2. In a small bowl, add 1 cup hot cream mixture to egg yolks, whisking until smooth. Add egg yolk mixture back to skillet, whisking until smooth. Add lobster, sherry, lemon juice, and salt. Cook for 3 to 4 minutes, stirring frequently, until lobster is firm and pink.

Roaring Twenties Roasted Caesar Salad
Makes 8 servings

- 4   small romaine hearts, split in half lengthwise
- ¼   cup olive oil
- 2   tablespoons fresh lemon juice
- 1½ teaspoons salt, divided
- 1   teaspoon garlic powder
- ¾   teaspoon ground black pepper, divided
- 2   cups panko (Japanese bread crumbs)
- 2   cups freshly grated Parmesan cheese
- 3   tablespoons chopped fresh parsley
- 6   tablespoons butter, melted

Classic Roasted Red Potatoes
Makes 8 servings

- 4   pounds red potatoes, cut into 1-inch pieces
- 3   tablespoons olive oil
- 1   tablespoon garlic powder
- 1½ teaspoons salt
- ½   teaspoon ground black pepper
- ¼   cup butter, melted
- ¼   cup chopped fresh parsley

1. Preheat oven to 400°. Line a large shallow roasting pan with foil.

2. In a large bowl, combine potatoes, olive oil, garlic powder, salt, and pepper, tossing to coat. Arrange potatoes in a single layer in prepared pan. Bake for 40 to 45 minutes or until potatoes are tender, stirring occasionally. Toss potatoes with melted butter and parsley.

Speakeasy Shrimp with Lindy Hoppin' John Cocktail Relish

Makes 10 to 12 servings

    3   quarts water
    1   (3-ounce) box dry shrimp and crab boil
    ¼   cup liquid shrimp and crab boil
    1   lemon, sliced
    3   tablespoons salt
    3   pounds large fresh shrimp
        Lindy Hoppin' John Cocktail Relish
          (recipe follows)
        Garnish: lemon slices

1. In a large Dutch oven, combine water, dry shrimp and crab boil, liquid shrimp and crab boil, lemon slices, and salt over medium-high heat. Bring to a boil, add shrimp, and return to a boil for 1 minute. Remove from heat, and let stand for 5 minutes.

2. Drain shrimp, and place in an ice bath until well chilled. Serve with Lindy Hoppin' John Cocktail Relish. Garnish with lemon slices, if desired.

LINDY HOPPIN' JOHN COCKTAIL RELISH

Makes 3 cups

    1   (15.8-ounce) can black-eyed peas,
          rinsed and drained
    1   cup seeded chopped tomato
    ¾   cup ketchup
    ½   cup chopped green onion
    ¼   cup finely chopped celery
    ¼   cup finely chopped red bell pepper
    3   tablespoons prepared horseradish
    ½   teaspoon salt
    ½   teaspoon garlic powder
    6   slices bacon, cooked and crumbled

1. In a medium bowl, combine black-eyed peas, tomato, ketchup, green onion, celery, bell pepper, horseradish, salt, and garlic powder, stirring to combine well. When ready to serve, stir in bacon.

Jazz Age Bread Pudding

Makes 12 servings

    2   (12-ounce) loaves French bread,
          cut into 1-inch pieces
    1½ cups chopped walnuts
    1   cup butter, melted
    1½ cups milk
    1   cup heavy whipping cream
    ¾   cup firmly packed dark brown sugar
    ½   cup granulated sugar
    1   tablespoon vanilla extract
    5   large eggs, lightly beaten
        Caramel Bourbon Sauce
          (recipe follows)

1. Preheat oven to 350°. Spray a 13x9-inch baking dish with cooking spray; set aside.

2. In a large bowl, combine bread, walnuts, and melted butter, tossing to combine.

3. In a large saucepan, combine milk, cream, brown sugar, granulated sugar, and vanilla. Bring to a simmer over medium heat, stirring frequently, until sugar dissolves. Remove from heat. Whisking constantly, slowly add eggs to hot milk mixture until smooth. Pour custard mixture over bread mixture; let stand for 10 minutes.

4. Pour bread mixture into prepared pan, and place in another, larger pan. Pour enough hot water into larger pan to reach halfway up sides of baking dish. Bake for 45 minutes; loosely cover with foil, and bake 30 more minutes or until custard is set and bread is golden brown. Remove from hot-water bath. Serve warm with Caramel Bourbon Sauce.

CARAMEL BOURBON SAUCE

Makes about 3 cups

    1¾ cups heavy whipping cream
    ½   cup bourbon
    ½   cup firmly packed dark brown sugar
    ½   cup butter, cut into pieces
    1   teaspoon vanilla extract

1. In a medium bowl, combine cream and bourbon. Bring to a simmer over medium heat, whisking constantly. Add brown sugar, reduce heat to medium-low, and simmer for 30 minutes or until slightly thickened. Remove from heat, and gradually whisk in butter until smooth. Stir in vanilla. Let cool slightly before serving.

Dinner Dressed Up

When the season's first chill settles in the air, retreat indoors for a bountiful spread that promises to warm spirits from within.

This visually splendid scene is rooted in a palette that echoes emblazoned leaves against a deep-blue sky. Fine china bearing a seasonal motif breathes elegance into the setting, while woven chargers and other stoneware pieces keep the overall mood casual. Bittersweet branches, pumpkins, and gourds piled into a dough bowl are just right for the centerpiece, and a miniature pumpkin placed at each seat offers an endearing personal touch.

menu

Autumn Salad with
Apple Cider Vinaigrette

Herb-Cheese Spread

Beef Stew with Red Wine
and Mushrooms

Butternut Squash Bowls

Buttercup-Gingersnap Tarts

Rum Coffee

Autumn Salad with Apple Cider Vinaigrette

Makes 6 servings

- ½ cup apple cider vinegar
- 2 teaspoons sugar
- ¼ teaspoon salt
- 1 large golden beet, peeled and thinly sliced
- 1 medium head radicchio, torn
- 1 (5-ounce) container arugula
- ½ cup pomegranate seeds
- Apple Cider Vinaigrette (recipe follows)

1. In a medium saucepan, bring vinegar, sugar, and salt to a boil.

2. In a medium bowl, place beet slices. Pour vinegar mixture over beets. Cover, and refrigerate for at least 2 hours or overnight. Drain beets.

3. In a large bowl, combine beets, radicchio, arugula, and pomegranate seeds. Add Apple Cider Vinaigrette; toss.

APPLE CIDER VINAIGRETTE
Makes ½ cup

- ¼ cup apple cider
- 2 tablespoons canola oil
- 1 tablespoon spicy brown mustard
- 1 tablespoon apple cider vinegar
- ¼ teaspoon salt
- ¼ teaspoon ground black pepper

1. In a medium bowl, whisk together apple cider, oil, mustard, vinegar, salt, and pepper.

Herb-Cheese Spread
Makes 1 cup

- 1 (8-ounce) package cream cheese, softened
- 2 tablespoons freshly grated Parmesan cheese
- 2 tablespoons minced fresh rosemary
- 2 tablespoons minced fresh sage
- 1 tablespoon whole milk
- ¼ teaspoon garlic powder
- ¼ teaspoon ground black pepper
- Toasted French bread slices, for serving

1. In a medium bowl, combine cheeses, rosemary, sage, milk, garlic powder, and pepper. Beat with a mixer at medium speed until blended. Serve with French bread.

Beef Stew with Red Wine and Mushrooms
Makes 6 servings

- 3 tablespoons vegetable oil, divided
- 2 cups chopped onion
- 1 cup chopped celery
- 1½ pounds sirloin steak, cut into 1-inch pieces
- 2 teaspoons salt, divided
- 1 teaspoon ground black pepper, divided
- 2 cups beef broth
- ½ cup dry red wine (such as Cabernet Sauvignon)
- 3 bay leaves
- 1 (14.5-ounce) can diced tomatoes, drained
- 1 (8-ounce) package whole white mushrooms, quartered
- 1 cup coarsely chopped carrots
- 2 tablespoons chopped fresh parsley
- 1 tablespoon fresh thyme
- 2 tablespoons all-purpose flour
- 3 tablespoons water
- 1 tablespoon red wine vinegar
- Butternut Squash Bowls (recipe follows)
- Garnish: thyme sprigs

1. In a medium Dutch oven, heat 1 tablespoon oil over medium-high heat. Add onion and celery to pan; cook for 2 minutes or until vegetables begin to soften. Remove from pan, and set aside. Heat remaining 2 tablespoons oil in pan.

2. Season beef with 1 teaspoon salt and ½ teaspoon pepper. Add half of beef to pan; cook for 3 minutes or until browned, turning occasionally. Remove from pan. Repeat procedure with remaining beef. Return onion mixture and beef to pan. Add broth, wine, bay leaves, tomatoes, and mushrooms. Cover, and simmer over medium-low heat for 1 hour or until beef is almost tender. Stir in remaining 1 teaspoon salt, remaining ½ teaspoon pepper, carrots, parsley, and thyme. Cover, and simmer for 30 minutes or until beef and carrots are tender.

3. In a small bowl, place flour; whisk in water. Stir into beef mixture. Bring to a boil over medium-high heat. Reduce heat to medium-low; cook for 3 minutes or until thickened. Stir in vinegar. Discard bay leaves. Serve stew in Butternut Squash Bowls. Garnish with thyme sprigs, if desired.

BUTTERNUT SQUASH BOWLS
Makes 6 bowls

- 6 medium butternut squash
- 1 tablespoon vegetable oil
- ½ teaspoon salt

1. Preheat oven to 350°. Spray a large rimmed baking sheet with cooking spray. Set aside.

2. Remove narrow portion of each squash; reserve for another use. Discard seeds from squash. Brush inside of squash with oil, and sprinkle with salt. Place squash cut side down on prepared pan. Bake for 25 minutes or until a knife can be easily inserted into squash.

Note: Choose squash that are about 4½ to 5 inches at the base.

Butterscotch-Gingersnap Tarts

Makes 6 tarts

- 48   gingersnap cookies*, finely ground
- 10   tablespoons unsalted butter, melted
- 2   teaspoons sugar
- 1   (3.4-ounce) box butterscotch instant pudding and pie mix
- 2   cups cold whole milk
- ½   cup frozen whipped topping, thawed
- Buttered Pecans (recipe follows)

1. Spray 6 (4-inch) tart pans with removable bottoms with cooking spray. Set aside.

2. In a medium bowl, combine ground gingersnap cookies, 8 tablespoons melted butter, and sugar until moistened. Add remaining 2 tablespoons butter if needed. Divide cookie mixture among tart pans, pressing with the back of a spoon or bottom of a plastic cup. Place on a rimmed baking sheet. Refrigerate for 30 minutes.

3. In a medium bowl, beat pudding mix and cold milk with a whisk for 2 minutes. Gently whisk in whipped topping. Spoon pudding into prepared gingersnap crusts. Refrigerate for at least 3 hours or overnight. Sprinkle with Buttered Pecans.

We used Nabisco Gingersnap Cookies.

BUTTERED PECANS
Makes ½ cup

- 1   tablespoon unsalted butter
- ½   cup chopped pecans
- ¼   teaspoon salt

1. In a small skillet, melt butter over medium heat. Add pecans; cook for 3 to 5 minutes or until toasted, stirring occasionally. Spoon pecans onto a paper towel; sprinkle with salt.

Rum Coffee

Makes 6 servings

- 6   cups boiling water
- 3   tablespoons espresso powder
- 6   tablespoons spiced rum
- 2   tablespoons sugar
- 6   tablespoons frozen whipped topping, thawed
- 6   tablespoons butterscotch sauce

1. In a small pitcher, combine boiling water, espresso powder, rum, and sugar, stirring until sugar and espresso powder are dissolved. Pour into serving cups. Top each serving with 1 tablespoon whipped topping and 1 tablespoon butterscotch sauce.

Christmas Sparkle

'Tis the season for festive gatherings with cherished loved ones and exquisite food.

The warm glow of candlelight shimmers across this inviting table set with rich reds and glittering metallics. Classic gold-trimmed white dinnerware and sophisticated crystal glasses elegantly anchor the arrangement, while lush florals and greenery incorporate natural beauty into the space. The nearby red-and-gold-festooned tree mimics the look of the table setting and evokes evergreen-scented memories of Christmases past.

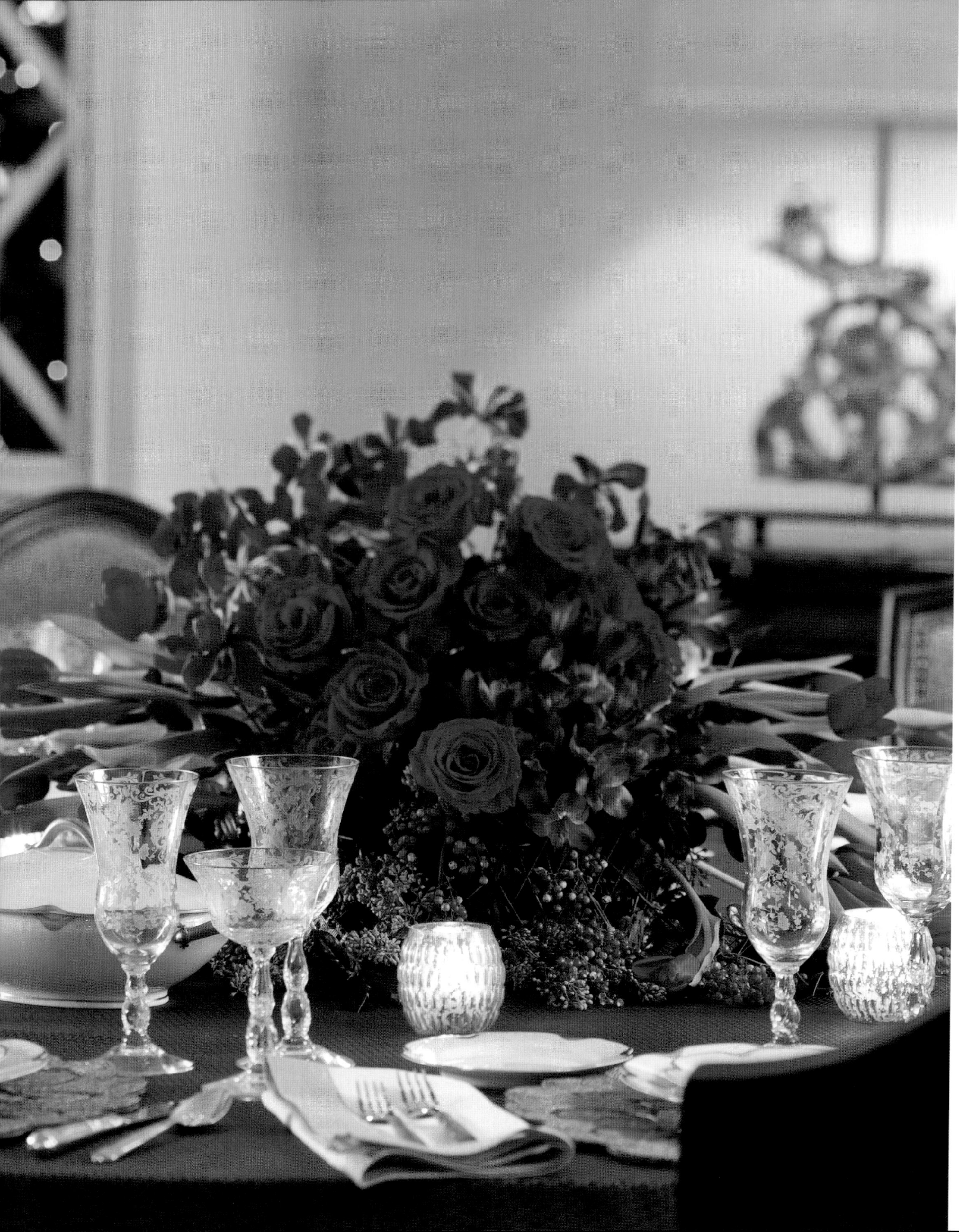

Cloverleaf Rolls

Makes 2 dozen

- 2 (0.25-ounce) packages active dry yeast
- ½ cup sugar, divided
- 2 cups warm milk (105° to 110°)
- 7 to 8 cups all-purpose flour
- 1½ tablespoons salt
- ½ cup vegetable oil
- ½ cup butter, melted
- 2 large eggs, lightly beaten

1. In a small bowl, combine yeast, ¼ cup sugar, and warm milk; let stand for 5 minutes.

2. In another small bowl, combine flour, remaining ¼ cup sugar, and salt.

3. In the bowl of a stand mixer fitted with a dough hook, combine milk mixture, oil, melted butter, and eggs. Gradually add flour mixture to milk mixture until a soft dough forms.

4. Turn out dough onto a lightly floured surface; knead until smooth and elastic, about 5 minutes. Place dough in a large greased bowl, turning to grease top. Loosely cover, and let rise in a warm place (85°), free from drafts, for 1 to 1½ hours or until doubled in size. Punch dough down; cover, and let stand for 10 minutes.

5. Grease 2 (12-cup) muffin pans. Shape dough into 1-inch balls, and place 3 dough balls in each muffin cup. Cover, and let rise in a warm place (85°), free from drafts, for 1 to 1½ hours or until doubled in size.

6. Preheat oven to 350°.

7. Bake for 15 minutes or until lightly browned.

Standing Rib Roast with Mushroom Sauce

Makes 8 to 10 servings

- 1 (9- to 10-pound) 4-rib roast
- 2 tablespoons olive oil
- 1 tablespoon onion powder
- 1 tablespoon garlic powder
- ½ teaspoon ground black pepper
- Mushroom Sauce (recipe follows)

1. Preheat oven to 450°. Line a roasting pan with heavy-duty foil.

2. Rub roast with olive oil.

3. In a small bowl, combine onion powder, garlic powder, and pepper. Rub entire roast with spice mixture. Place roast, rib side down, in prepared pan. Bake for 15 minutes; reduce oven temperature to 325°, and bake for 2 hours to 2 hours and 15 minutes or until a meat thermometer inserted in center registers 120° or desired temperature. Cover loosely with foil, and let stand for 15 to 20 minutes. Serve with Mushroom Sauce.

MUSHROOM SAUCE

Makes 8 to 10 servings

- ¼ cup olive oil
- 2 (8-ounce) containers sliced baby portobello mushrooms
- 1 large yellow onion, chopped
- 1 tablespoon minced garlic
- 1 teaspoon garlic powder
- ½ teaspoon salt
- ½ teaspoon ground black pepper
- 2 tablespoons all-purpose flour
- ¼ cup dry red wine
- 2 (10.5-ounce) cans beef consommé
- 2 tablespoons Worcestershire sauce
- 2 tablespoons cold butter, cut into pieces

menu

Cloverleaf Rolls

Standing Rib Roast with
Mushroom Sauce

Sautéed Kale

Parmesan Truffle
Mashed Potatoes

Roasted Herbed Carrots

Crème Brûlée Cheesecake

Add kale; cook for 2 minutes, stirring frequently. Add chicken broth, vinegar, brown sugar, remaining 1½ teaspoons salt, garlic powder, onion powder, and pepper. Cook for 5 minutes, stirring frequently.

Parmesan Truffle Mashed Potatoes
Makes 8 to 10 servings

- 4 quarts water
- 1 tablespoon plus 1 teaspoon salt, divided
- 2 pounds Yukon gold potatoes, cubed
- 2 pounds red potatoes, cubed
- 1 cup sour cream
- ½ cup butter, softened
- 3 cups finely grated Parmesan cheese
- ¼ cup white truffle oil
- 1 tablespoon chopped fresh parsley
- ½ teaspoon ground black pepper

1. In a large Dutch oven, combine water, 1 tablespoon salt, and potatoes over medium-high heat. Bring to a boil; cook for 10 to 15 minutes or until tender.

2. Drain potatoes well, and return to saucepan. Add sour cream and butter. Using a potato masher, mash potato mixture until butter melts. Add Parmesan cheese, truffle oil, parsley, remaining 1 teaspoon salt, and pepper, stirring to combine well.

Roasted Herbed Carrots
Makes 8 to 10 servings

- 6 (6-ounce) bags rainbow baby carrots, halved lengthwise
- 2 shallots, thinly sliced
- 3 tablespoons olive oil
- 2 tablespoons chopped fresh thyme
- 1½ tablespoons chopped fresh rosemary
- 1 tablespoon minced garlic
- 1 teaspoon salt
- ¾ teaspoon ground black pepper

1. In a large skillet, heat olive oil over medium heat. Add mushrooms, onion, garlic, garlic powder, salt, and pepper; cook for 20 minutes, stirring occasionally. Add flour; cook for 2 minutes, stirring constantly. Add wine; cook for 2 minutes, stirring constantly. Gradually add consommé and Worcestershire sauce, stirring until smooth. Simmer for 5 minutes. Stir in butter, a little at a time, until melted.

Sautéed Kale
Makes 8 to 10 servings

- 4 quarts water
- 1 tablespoon plus 1½ teaspoons salt, divided
- 2 heads kale, chopped
- ¼ cup olive oil
- 1 large yellow onion, thinly sliced
- 1 tablespoon minced garlic
- ¾ cup chicken broth
- ½ cup apple cider vinegar
- 1 tablespoon firmly packed dark brown sugar
- 1 teaspoon garlic powder
- 1 teaspoon onion powder
- ½ teaspoon ground black pepper

1. In a large Dutch oven, bring water and 1 tablespoon salt to a boil over medium-high heat. Add kale; cook for 3 minutes, stirring occasionally. Remove from heat, and drain thoroughly; set aside.

2. In Dutch oven, heat olive oil over medium-high heat. Add onion; cook for 5 to 6 minutes, stirring constantly. Add minced garlic; cook for 1 minute, stirring constantly.

1. Preheat oven to 450°. Line a rimmed baking sheet with foil; set aside.

2. In a large bowl, combine carrots, shallot, olive oil, thyme, rosemary, garlic, salt, and pepper, tossing to combine well. Arrange carrots in an even layer in prepared pan. Bake for 15 minutes or until crisp tender.

Crème Brûlée Cheesecake

Makes 1 (9-inch) cheesecake

Crust:

2	cups firmly packed vanilla wafer crumbs
⅓	cup sugar
6	tablespoons butter, melted
1	large egg white, lightly beaten

Filling:

4	(8-ounce) packages cream cheese, softened
1½	cups plus ¼ cup sugar, divided
6	large egg yolks
2	tablespoons all-purpose flour
1	cup sour cream

Garnish: sugared fresh raspberries

1. Preheat oven to 300°.

2. For crust: In a small bowl, combine vanilla wafer crumbs, ⅓ cup sugar, melted butter, and egg white, stirring to combine well. Press firmly on bottom and up sides of a 9 ½-inch springform pan. Bake for 8 minutes; set aside to let cool.

3. For filling: In a large bowl, beat cream cheese and 1 ½ cups sugar with a mixer at medium speed until fluffy. Beat in egg yolks, one at a time, beating well after each addition. Add flour, beating just until combined. Stir in sour cream. Spoon batter into prepared crust. Bake for 1 hour and 15 minutes; turn oven off. Leave in oven with door closed for 4 hours. Remove cheesecake from oven. Gently run a knife around edge of pan to release sides. Let cool completely in pan. Cover, and refrigerate for 8 hours.

4. Evenly sprinkle remaining ¼ cup sugar on top of cheesecake. Caramelize sugar with kitchen torch until sugar is melted. Remove sides of pan to serve. Garnish with sugared fresh raspberries, if desired.

Holiday Dinner

Bring together kith and kin for a delicious Yuletide meal, filled with the flavors of the season.

Dinnerware in the classic Holiday pattern by Lenox forms the foundation for this seasonal setting. The china's holly motif is repeated in the crystal. In lieu of a traditional centerpiece, create a floral runner of white roses and greenery.

Caramelized Onion Dip
with Tarragon

Maple and Mustard
Glazed Ham

Holiday Haricots Verts

Potatoes Au Gratin

Buttery Herbed Crescent Rolls

Chocolate Pecan Pie

Vanilla Bean Cake
with Cinnamon Filling
and Caramel Icing

Caramelized Onion Dip with Tarragon

Makes 6 cups

¼ cup butter
4 shallots, thinly sliced
3 large red onions, sliced ⅛ inch thick
3 tablespoons tarragon vinegar
1 tablespoon minced garlic
1 teaspoon salt
½ teaspoon ground black pepper
2 (8-ounce) packages cream cheese, softened
1 (16-ounce) container sour cream
3 cups freshly grated Parmesan cheese, divided
3 tablespoons chopped fresh tarragon
Garnish: chopped fresh tarragon

1. Preheat oven to 350°. Lightly grease a 1½-quart baking dish with cooking spray.

2. In a large Dutch oven, melt butter over medium-low heat. Add shallot and onion; cover, and cook for 30 minutes, stirring occasionally. Remove cover, and increase heat to medium-high; cook for 10 to 12 minutes, stirring occasionally. Add vinegar, garlic, salt, and pepper. Cook for 1 to 2 minutes or until vinegar evaporates. Reduce heat to low. Add cream cheese, sour cream, 2 cups Parmesan cheese, and tarragon, stirring until cheese melts. Spoon onion mixture into prepared pan, and top with remaining 1 cup Parmesan cheese. Bake for 30 minutes or until browned and bubbly. Garnish with tarragon, if desired. Serve with pita chips or crackers.

Maple and Mustard Glazed Ham

Makes 12 servings

1 cup firmly packed light brown sugar
6 tablespoons whole-grain mustard
¼ cup maple syrup
1 tablespoon smoked paprika
2 teaspoons Worcestershire sauce
1 teaspoon garlic powder
1 (12-pound) shank-portion fully cooked smoked ham

1. Preheat oven to 325°. Line a roasting pan with foil.

2. In a small bowl, combine brown sugar, mustard, maple syrup, smoked paprika, Worcestershire sauce, and garlic powder, whisking to combine; set aside.

3. Place ham in prepared pan. Cover with foil; bake for 3 hours. Remove foil, and continue baking for 1 hour or until a meat thermometer inserted in center registers 150°, basting ham with glaze every 15 minutes.

Holiday Haricots Verts
Makes 10 to 12 servings

- 1 tablespoon olive oil
- 1 pound hickory-smoked bacon, cut into 1-inch pieces
- 1 large yellow onion, thinly sliced
- 1 tablespoon minced garlic
- 4 pounds haricots verts
- 3 quarts chicken broth
- 1 tablespoon sugar
- 2 teaspoons salt
- 1 teaspoon garlic powder
- ½ teaspoon ground black pepper

1. In a large Dutch oven, heat olive oil over medium-high heat. Add bacon; cook for 8 to 10 minutes, stirring frequently, until browned and crisp. Add onion and garlic; cook for 2 to 3 minutes, stirring constantly. Add haricots verts, chicken broth, sugar, salt, garlic powder, and pepper, stirring to combine. Bring to a simmer. Reduce heat to medium, and cook, uncovered, for 2 hours, stirring occasionally.

Potatoes Au Gratin
Makes 10 to 12 servings

- 1 cup heavy whipping cream
- 1½ teaspoons salt
- 1 teaspoon garlic powder
- ½ teaspoon ground black pepper
- 3 pounds thinly sliced red potatoes
- 2 cups shredded fontina cheese
- 2 cups shredded smoked Gouda cheese
- 2 cups shredded Monterey Jack cheese

Garnish: chopped fresh parsley

1. Preheat oven to 400°. Lightly grease a 13x9-inch baking dish with cooking spray.

2. In a small bowl, whisk together cream, salt, garlic powder, and pepper.

3. In prepared pan, layer half of potatoes, half of cheese, and half of cream mixture; repeat layers. Place on a baking sheet. Cover with foil, and bake for 1 hour and 40 minutes. Remove foil, and continue baking for 15 to 20 minutes or until potatoes are tender and cheese is lightly browned. Let stand for 15 minutes before serving. Garnish with parsley, if desired.

Chocolate Pecan Pie

Makes 1 (9-inch) deep-dish pie

- ½ (14.1-ounce) package refrigerated pie crust
- 1 cup firmly packed light brown sugar
- ½ cup light corn syrup
- ½ cup dark corn syrup
- ¼ cup butter, melted
- 3 large eggs
- 1½ teaspoons vanilla extract
- ¼ teaspoon salt
- 2½ cups chopped pecans
- 1 (12-ounce) bag mini semisweet chocolate morsels

1. Preheat oven to 350°.

2. On a lightly floured surface, roll pastry to a 12-inch circle. Fit pie crust into a 9-inch deep-dish pie plate. Trim excess pastry ½ inch beyond edge of pie plate. Fold edges under, and crimp. Cover bottom of pastry with pie weights. Bake for 8 minutes; remove pie weights, and set aside.

3. In a large bowl, combine brown sugar and corn syrups. Whisk in melted butter and eggs until well combined. Whisk in vanilla and salt. Stir in pecans and chocolate morsels. Spoon pecan mixture into prepared crust. Bake for 35 minutes or until center is set.

Buttery Herbed Crescent Rolls

Makes 16 rolls

- ¾ cup butter, softened
- 1½ tablespoons chopped fresh rosemary
- 1½ tablespoons chopped fresh thyme
- 1½ tablespoons chopped fresh chives
- 1½ tablespoons chopped fresh parsley
- ½ teaspoon garlic powder
- ¼ teaspoon ground black pepper
- 2 (12-ounce) cans refrigerated crescent roll dough*

Garnish: garlic powder

1. Preheat oven to 350°. Line a rimmed baking sheet with parchment paper.

2. In a small bowl, combine butter, rosemary, thyme, chives, parsley, garlic powder, and pepper, stirring well to combine.

3. Separate crescent dough into triangles. Spoon about 1 teaspoon butter mixture at the base of each triangle, and roll up, crescent style. Place on prepared pan. Garnish with garlic powder, if desired. Bake for 12 to 15 minutes or until lightly browned.

We used Pillsbury Grands Crescent Big and Flaky.

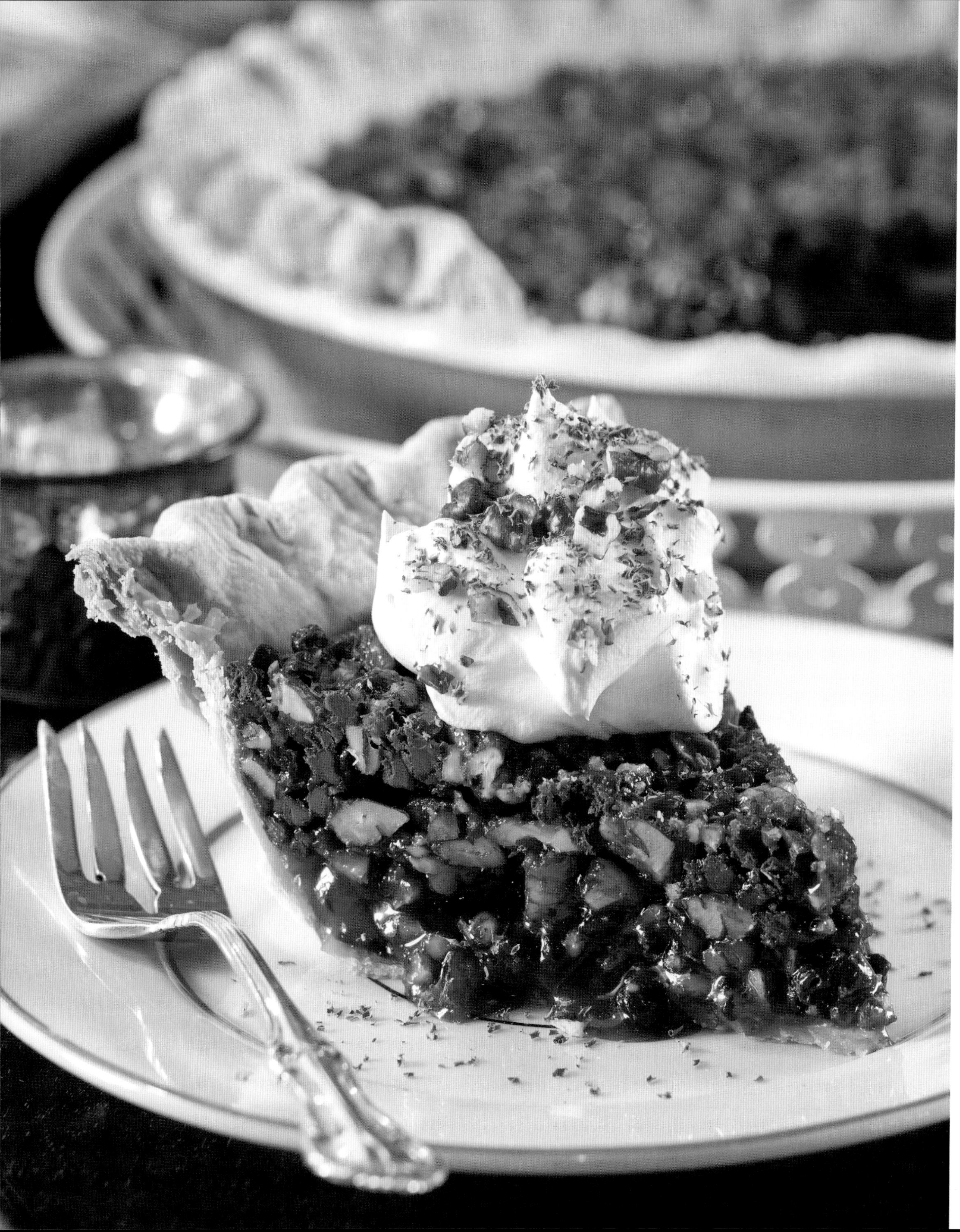

Vanilla Bean Cake with Cinnamon Filling and Caramel Icing

Makes 1 (9-inch) cake

1½ cups butter, softened
2 cups sugar
4 large eggs
1 vanilla bean, split and scraped, seeds reserved
½ teaspoon vanilla extract
2½ cups all-purpose flour
2 teaspoons baking powder
¼ teaspoon salt
1 cup whole buttermilk
Cinnamon Filling (recipe follows)
Caramel Icing (recipe follows)
Sweet and Salty Pecans (recipe follows)

1. Preheat oven to 350°. Spray 3 (9-inch) round cake pans with baking spray with flour.

2. In a medium bowl, beat butter and sugar with a mixer at medium speed until fluffy. Add eggs, one at a time, beating well after each addition. Beat in vanilla bean seeds and vanilla.

3. In a medium bowl, combine flour, baking powder, and salt. Gradually add flour mixture to butter mixture alternately with buttermilk, beginning and ending with flour mixture. Spoon batter into prepared pans. Bake for 20 to 25 minutes or until a wooden pick inserted in center comes out clean. Let cool in pans for 10 minutes. Remove from pans, and let cool completely on wire racks.

4. Spread Cinnamon Filling between layers. Spread Caramel Icing on top and sides of cake. Top with Sweet and Salty Pecans.

CINNAMON FILLING
Makes about 3 cups

½ cup butter, softened
1 (8-ounce) package cream cheese, softened
1 teaspoon ground cinnamon
3 cups confectioners' sugar
1 teaspoon vanilla extract

1. In a medium bowl, combine butter, cream cheese, and cinnamon. Beat with a mixer at medium speed until smooth. Gradually add confectioners' sugar, beating until smooth. Beat in vanilla.

CARAMEL ICING
Makes about 5 cups

1 cup butter, cut into pieces
2 cups firmly packed dark brown sugar
1 teaspoon salt
1 cup sour cream, room temperature
5 cups confectioners' sugar, sifted
1 teaspoon vanilla extract

1. In a large saucepan, bring butter, brown sugar, and salt to a boil over medium heat, stirring constantly. Remove from heat; slowly stir in sour cream.

2. Return mixture to medium heat, and bring just to a boil, stirring constantly. Remove from heat. Gradually add confectioners' sugar, beating with a mixer at medium speed until smooth. Beat in vanilla. Let stand for 20 minutes or until mixture is a spreadable consistency.

SWEET AND SALTY PECANS
Makes 2 cups

¼ cup butter
¼ cup honey
2 tablespoons firmly packed dark brown sugar
½ teaspoon salt
2 cups chopped pecans
Coarse kosher salt

1. Preheat oven to 275°. Line a baking sheet with parchment paper.

2. In a medium bowl, combine butter, honey, brown sugar, and salt. Microwave on high in 30-second intervals, stirring between each, until melted and smooth (about 1 minute). Add pecans, tossing to coat. Spread pecans in an even layer on prepared pan. Bake for 10 to 12 minutes. Remove from oven, and sprinkle with kosher salt. Let cool completely on pan. Break into pieces.

A Winter's Repast

The fire roars, the table shimmers with china and crystal—what a lovely scene
for a winter dinner shared with dearest friends.

Camembert with
Roasted Grapes

Beef Tenderloin Medallions
with Madeira Sauce

Brussels Sprouts with
Bacon and Apple

Parmesan-Chive
Scalloped Potatoes

Cream Cheese and Chive
Crescent Rolls

Triple-Chocolate
Almond Decadence

"Winter is the time for comfort, for good food and warmth, for the touch of a friendly hand and for a talk beside the fire: it is the time for home."

—Edith Sitwell

Camembert with Roasted Grapes
Makes 6 servings

1 (8-ounce) round Camembert cheese
2½ cups red seedless grapes
2 tablespoons extra-virgin olive oil
½ teaspoon salt
½ teaspoon ground black pepper
 Flatbread crackers

1. Let Camembert sit at room temperature for 30 minutes.

2. Preheat oven to 400°.

3. Line a rimmed baking sheet with foil. Spread grapes in an even layer on prepared pan. Drizzle with olive oil; sprinkle with salt and pepper, stirring to coat. Bake for 20 to 25 minutes or until grapes begin to burst but not burn. Let rest for at least 5 minutes (grapes will be very hot inside).

4. Place cheese on a serving dish. Spoon grapes over cheese. Let rest for 5 minutes before serving. Serve with flatbread crackers.

Beef Tenderloin Medallions with Madeira Sauce
Makes 6 servings

2½ pounds trimmed beef tenderloin
3 tablespoons vegetable oil
1 teaspoon salt
1 teaspoon ground black pepper
1 cup Madeira wine
1 shallot, minced
3 tablespoons butter, cut into
3 pieces

1. Preheat oven to 350°.

2. Heat an ovenproof skillet over medium-high heat.

3. Rub tenderloin with oil; sprinkle with salt and pepper. Cook tenderloin in skillet for 2 to 3 minutes per side or until browned. Transfer skillet to oven. Bake for 15 to 20 minutes or until a thermometer inserted in the thickest part of the tenderloin registers 135° or desired degree of doneness.

4. Remove tenderloin from skillet, and place on a cutting board. Let meat rest for 15 minutes before cutting into 6 equal portions.

5. In a medium saucepan, combine Madeira and shallot. Cook over medium-high heat, stirring frequently, for 10 minutes or until Madeira has reduced to approximately ¼ cup. Reduce heat to low. Add butter, stirring to melt. Serve sauce with tenderloin.

Brussels Sprouts with Bacon and Apple
Makes 6 servings

1½	pounds Brussels sprouts
6	slices bacon
1	large Braeburn apple
¼	cup firmly packed light brown sugar
1½	tablespoons cider vinegar
½	teaspoon salt
½	teaspoon ground black pepper

1. Trim ends of Brussels sprouts, and finely slice. Rinse Brussels sprouts in a colander, and pat dry.

2. In a large nonstick skillet, cook bacon over medium heat for 4 to 6 minutes or until crispy. Place bacon on paper towels to drain. Crumble bacon. Drain grease from pan, reserving 3 tablespoons.

3. Core apple, and slice into bite-size pieces.

4. In a small bowl, whisk together brown sugar, vinegar, salt, and pepper.

5. Heat reserved bacon grease in skillet over medium-high heat. Add Brussels sprouts, and cook for 3 to 4 minutes or until they begin to brown slightly, stirring often. Add apple to skillet, stirring to combine; cook for 1 minute. Pour brown sugar mixture over sprouts mixture. Cook for 1 minute or until sugar has dissolved, stirring often. Add bacon, stirring to combine.

Parmesan-Chive Scalloped Potatoes
Makes 6 servings

3	medium to large Yukon gold potatoes
¼	cup plus 2 tablespoons butter, divided
¼	cup all-purpose flour
1⅓	cups whole milk
1	teaspoon salt, divided

1	teaspoon ground black pepper, divided
3	tablespoons chopped chives, divided
1	cup grated Parmesan cheese, divided
⅔	cup panko (Japanese bread crumbs)

1. Preheat oven to 350°. Spray a 2-quart baking dish with cooking spray.

2. Peel and thinly slice potatoes.

3. In a large nonstick saucepan, melt ¼ cup butter over medium heat. Sift flour over butter, whisking to combine. Cook flour mixture for 2 to 3 minutes or until thickened, whisking well. Slowly add milk, whisking to combine. Cook for 5 minutes or until thickened, whisking frequently. Add ¾ teaspoon salt and ¾ teaspoon pepper, whisking well.

4. Spread ¼ cup milk mixture over bottom of prepared pan. Layer half of potatoes evenly in a circular pattern over milk mixture. Spread half of remaining milk mixture over potatoes. Top with 1 tablespoon chopped chives and ½ cup grated Parmesan cheese. Repeat layers with remaining potatoes, milk mixture, and 1 tablespoon chopped chives.

5. Microwave remaining 2 tablespoons butter in a microwave-safe bowl for 30 seconds or until melted. Combine butter, panko, remaining ½ cup grated Parmesan, remaining ¼ teaspoon salt, and remaining ¼ teaspoon pepper in a medium bowl. Spread over potatoes. Cover, and bake for 45 minutes. Remove cover, and bake for 15 minutes or until golden brown. Top with remaining 1 tablespoon chives. Let stand for 10 minutes before serving.

Cream Cheese and Chive Crescent Rolls

Makes 8 crescent rolls

- 4   ounces cream cheese, softened
- 1   tablespoon chopped chives
- 1   (8-ounce) can refrigerated crescent roll dough

1. Preheat oven to 375°. Line a baking sheet with parchment paper.

2. In a medium bowl, combine cream cheese and chives. Divide into 8 equal portions.

3. Unroll 1 piece crescent dough. Place 1 portion cream cheese mixture in center of widest end of crescent dough. Roll dough over mixture from widest end to smallest. Place on prepared pan. Repeat with remaining dough and cream cheese mixture. Bake for 10 to 12 minutes or until lightly golden.

Triple Chocolate–Almond Decadence

Makes 6 servings

- 2   (19-ounce) boxes brownie mix*
- ⅓   cup sliced almonds
- 4   ounces white chocolate, finely chopped
- 1   (8-ounce) package cream cheese, softened
- ⅔   cup unsweetened cocoa powder
- ½   cup sugar
- ¾   cup Frangelico
- ½   cup water
- Garnish: fresh raspberries

1. Line 2 (9-inch) pans with foil; spray with baking spray.

2. Prepare and bake brownie mix according to package directions; let cool completely in pan. Remove brownie from pan. Cut into 9 (3-inch) circles. Cut circles in half horizontally.

3. Spread almonds in an even layer on a rimmed baking sheet. Bake at 350° for 4 to 7 minutes or until lightly golden. Remove from oven, and let cool completely on pan.

4. In a large microwave-safe bowl, microwave white chocolate in 30-second intervals until melted, stirring between each interval. Add cream cheese to melted white chocolate, stirring until smooth. Spoon cream cheese mixture into piping bag fitted with a large round tip.

5. In a medium saucepan, combine cocoa powder, sugar, Frangelico, and water, whisking well. Bring to a boil over medium-high heat. Reduce heat to a low boil. Cook for 1 minute, whisking until smooth. Remove from heat, and let cool for 5 minutes.

6. Pipe cream cheese onto 2 brownie rounds. Stack rounds on top of each other, pressing gently. Gently press a third brownie round (no icing) cut side down on top of cream cheese mixture. Repeat with remaining brownie rounds and cream cheese mixture. Place on serving plates. Spoon chocolate Frangelico sauce over the top, and sprinkle with sliced almonds. Garnish with fresh raspberries, if desired.

We used Ghirardelli Chocolate Supreme Brownie Mix.

ENTERTAINING COOKBOOK

VOL. 2

Soirée
AWAY

Take the party to the patio and beyond, and enjoy the many vibrant settings dining outdoors offers.

Luncheon in the Garden

When gardens reach their peak of bloom and the season displays her brilliant finery, you need little more than a few simple, elegant touches to enhance an alfresco gathering.

"'Tis wealth enough
of joy for me
In summer time
to simply be."
—Paul Laurence Dunbar

Heirloom Tomato Salad with White Balsamic Dressing
Makes 6 to 8 servings

 2 red heirloom tomatoes, cut into
    1-inch pieces
 2 yellow heirloom tomatoes, cut into
    1-inch pieces
 2 green heirloom tomatoes, cut into
    1-inch pieces
 2 (8-ounce) containers fresh mini
    mozzarella balls, drained
 1 (1-ounce) package fresh basil,
    coarsely chopped
 White Balsamic Dressing (recipe
    follows)

1. In a medium bowl, combine tomatoes, mozzarella, and basil. Pour White Balsamic Dressing over tomato mixture. Cover, and refrigerate for at least 1 hour, stirring occasionally.

WHITE BALSAMIC DRESSING
Makes 1½ cups

1 cup white balsamic vinegar
½ teaspoon salt
½ teaspoon ground black pepper
½ cup extra-virgin olive oil

1. In a small bowl, combine vinegar, salt, and pepper, whisking to combine. In a slow, steady stream, gradually add olive oil, whisking to combine well.

Limoncello Spritzer
Makes about ½ gallon

 1 cup sugar
 1 cup water
 1 (750-milliliter) bottle Pinot
    Grigio, chilled
 1 (750-milliliter) bottle Prosecco,
    chilled
 1 cup Limoncello, chilled
 1 (10-ounce) bottle club soda
 Garnish: lemon wedges

1. In a small saucepan, combine sugar and water over medium-high heat, stirring constantly. Bring mixture to a boil; reduce heat to low, and simmer 3 to 4 minutes, stirring constantly. Remove from heat; let cool completely.

2. In a pitcher, combine Pinot Grigio, Prosecco, Limoncello, ¼ cup sugar syrup, and club soda, stirring gently to combine. Garnish with lemon wedges, if desired. Store remaining syrup in an airtight container in refrigerator for up to 3 weeks.

menu

Limoncello Spritzer

Heirloom Tomato Salad with
White Balsamic Dressing

Chicken Oscar

Classic Risotto

Strawberry Meringue
Ice Cream

Chicken Oscar
Makes 6 servings

Hollandaise Sauce (recipe follows)
1   (8-ounce) container jumbo lump crab meat, picked
2   tablespoons fresh lemon juice
1   tablespoon chopped fresh parsley
3   boneless skinless chicken breasts
1   cup all-purpose flour
1   teaspoon garlic powder
1   teaspoon onion powder
1½ teaspoons salt, divided
1   teaspoon ground black pepper, divided
¼   cup butter
3   tablespoons olive oil
18 asparagus spears, trimmed

1. Prepare Hollandaise Sauce; keep warm.

2. In a small bowl, combine crab meat, lemon juice, and parsley. Cover and refrigerate.

3. Preheat oven to 200°. Line a baking sheet with parchment paper; set aside.

4. Cut each chicken piece in half horizontally. Place chicken breasts between plastic wrap, and pound with a meat mallet to ⅛-inch thickness.

5. In a shallow dish, combine flour, garlic powder, onion powder, 1 teaspoon salt, and ½ teaspoon pepper. Coat chicken in flour mixture, shaking off excess.

6. In a large nonstick skillet, heat butter over medium-high heat. Cook chicken for 2 to 3 minutes per side or until lightly

browned. Place chicken on prepared pan, and place in oven.

7. Wipe out skillet. Return skillet to stove top over medium heat. Add olive oil, and heat over medium-high heat. Add asparagus, remaining ½ teaspoon salt, and remaining ½ teaspoon pepper. Cook for 4 to 5 minutes, stirring constantly, until crisp tender.

8. To serve, top each piece of chicken with Hollandaise Sauce, crab meat mixture, and asparagus.

HOLLANDAISE SAUCE
Makes about 1¼ cups

4   large egg yolks
2   tablespoons fresh lemon juice
2   teaspoons Dijon mustard
½   teaspoon Worcestershire sauce

1   teaspoon hot sauce
1   cup melted butter
2   tablespoons hot water
¼   teaspoon salt
¼   teaspoon ground black pepper

1. Fill the bottom of a double boiler with 1 inch of water; bring water to a simmer over medium-low heat. Place top of double boiler over simmering water. In the top of double boiler, whisk together egg yolks, lemon juice, mustard, Worcestershire sauce, and hot sauce. Whisking constantly, add melted butter, 2 tablespoons at a time, until all butter is incorporated. Whisk in water as needed to prevent sauce from becoming too thick. Remove from heat, and whisk in salt and pepper.

Classic Risotto
Makes 6 servings

4   tablespoons butter, divided
2   tablespoons olive oil
½   cup finely chopped green onion
1½ cups Arborio rice
¼   cup white wine
5   cups hot chicken broth
½   cup finely grated Parmigiano-Reggiano cheese
½   cup finely grated Gruyère cheese
¼   teaspoon ground black pepper

1. In a medium heavy-bottomed Dutch oven, heat 2 tablespoons butter and 2 tablespoons olive oil over medium heat until butter is melted. Add green onion; cook for 2 to 3 minutes or until tender. Add rice; cook for 2 to 3 minutes, stirring constantly, until very lightly browned. Add wine; cook for 2 minutes, stirring constantly. Add hot chicken broth, ½ cup at a time, allowing liquid to be absorbed after each addition, stirring constantly. Repeat procedure until rice becomes creamy in texture, about 25 to 30 minutes. Remove from heat, and add cheeses, pepper, and remaining 2 tablespoons butter, stirring until cheese is melted.

Strawberry Meringue Ice Cream
Makes about 2 quarts

2   cups heavy whipping cream
2   cups half-and-half
1½ cups sugar
4   large egg yolks
1   tablespoon strawberry extract
1   (1-pound) container fresh strawberries, pureed
1   (5-ounce) container vanilla meringue cookies, crumbled
Garnish: fresh strawberries, crushed meringue cookies

1. In a heavy 3-quart saucepan, combine cream, half-and-half, and sugar. Bring to a simmer over medium-low heat; do not boil.

2. In a small bowl, whisk together egg yolks and strawberry extract. Add 2 cups hot cream mixture to egg mixture, whisking to combine. Whisking constantly, gradually add egg mixture to remaining hot cream mixture. Increase to medium heat, and cook for 6 to 7 minutes, until mixture coats the back of a spoon. Remove from heat, and let cool for 10 minutes.

3. Strain mixture through a fine-mesh strainer into an airtight container. Whisk in strawberry purée. Cover, and refrigerate for 4 hours to overnight.

4. Pour ice cream mixture and meringues into an ice cream freezer. Freeze according to manufacturer's instructions. Ice cream will be soft. For firmer ice cream, place in an airtight container, and freeze for several hours or overnight. Garnish with strawberries and crushed cookies, if desired.

Simply Splendid

Wisteria perfumes the air as songbirds share their merry tunes—it's the ideal setting for a delicious afternoon lunch on the veranda.

Lemon Cucumber Tea

Makes about 1 gallon

- 3 quarts cold water, divided
- 3 family-size tea bags
- Lemon Cucumber Simple Syrup (recipe follows)
- 5 tablespoons fresh lemon juice
- Garnish: lemon slices, cucumber slices

1. In a medium saucepan, bring 1 quart water to a boil; remove from heat. Add tea bags; cover, and steep for 5 minutes. Strain tea into a large pitcher.

2. Add Lemon Cucumber Simple Syrup, lemon juice, and remaining 2 quarts water, stirring to mix well. Serve over ice. Garnish with lemon slices and cucumber slices, if desired.

LEMON CUCUMBER SIMPLE SYRUP
Makes about 2½ cups

- 2 cups water
- 2 cups sugar
- 2 tablespoons lemon zest
- 1 English cucumber, grated

1. In a medium saucepan, combine water and sugar over medium-high heat, stirring until sugar dissolves. Add lemon zest and cucumber. Bring to a boil, reduce heat to medium-low, and simmer for 15 minutes. Remove from heat.

2. Strain syrup, discarding solids. Let cool completely.

Grilled Chicken Salad with Grilled Peach Vinaigrette

Makes 6 servings

- 6 boneless skinless chicken breasts
- 1 teaspoon salt
- 1 teaspoon garlic powder
- ½ teaspoon ground black pepper
- 1 head green leaf lettuce, washed and torn
- 1 (4-ounce) bag watercress, stems removed
- 1 (4-ounce) bag arugula
- 6 small ripe peaches, pitted, sliced
- 2 pints fresh raspberries
- 1 cup toasted pecan halves
- 1 (4-ounce) container goat cheese crumbles
- Grilled Peach Vinaigrette (recipe follows)

1. Preheat oven to 200°.

2. Spray grill rack with nonflammable cooking spray. Preheat grill to medium-high heat (350° to 400°).

3. Evenly sprinkle both sides of chicken with salt, garlic powder, and pepper. Grill chicken, covered with grill lid, for 8 to 10 minutes per side or until a meat thermometer registers 165° or desired degree of doneness. Place in oven to keep warm.

4. On each of 6 salad plates, evenly divide lettuce, watercress, arugula, peaches, raspberries, pecans, and goat cheese. Slice grilled chicken, and place on top of salad. Serve with Grilled Peach Vinaigrette.

GRILLED PEACH VINAIGRETTE
Makes about 3½ cups

- 6 small ripe peaches, halved, pitted
- 2 tablespoons olive oil
- 2 (5.5-ounce) cans peach or apricot nectar
- 1 shallot, chopped
- ¼ cup Champagne vinegar
- ¾ teaspoon salt
- ½ teaspoon white pepper
- ½ cup extra-light olive oil

1. Spray grill rack with nonflammable cooking spray. Preheat grill to medium-high heat (350° to 400°).

2. In a medium bowl, combine peaches and olive oil, tossing to coat. Grill peach halves, covered with grill lid, for 1 to 2 minutes per side or until golden.

3. In the container of a blender, combine peaches, peach nectar, shallot, vinegar, salt, and pepper. Blend until smooth. With blender running, gradually add olive oil in a slow, steady stream.

menu

Lemon Cucumber Tea

Grilled Chicken Salad with
Grilled Peach Vinaigrette

Grilled Shrimp Cocktail with
Roasted Cocktail Sauce

Melon Salad

Coconut Cake

1 large yellow onion, thinly sliced
1 head garlic, cloves peeled
2 tablespoons olive oil
1¾ teaspoons salt, divided
½ teaspoon ground black pepper
3 tablespoons prepared horseradish
2 tablespoons Worcestershire sauce
2 tablespoons fresh lemon juice

1. Preheat oven to 400°. Line a rimmed baking sheet with foil.

2. In a large bowl, combine tomatoes, onion, garlic cloves, olive oil, 1 teaspoon salt, and pepper, tossing to coat. Spread tomato mixture in an even layer on prepared pan. Bake for 30 minutes. Let cool on pan for 10 minutes.

3. In the work bowl of a food processor or the container of a blender, combine tomato mixture, horseradish, Worcestershire sauce, lemon juice, and remaining ¾ teaspoon salt. Process until smooth.

Melon Salad
Makes 6 servings

1 seedless watermelon
1 cantaloupe
1 honeydew
1 tablespoon lime zest
¼ cup fresh lime juice
3 tablespoons honey
2 tablespoons Champagne vinegar
Garnish: chopped fresh mint

1. Using a melon baller, scoop 1-inch balls from melons, and combine in a large bowl.

2. In a small bowl, whisk together lime zest, lime juice, honey, and vinegar, whisking until honey dissolves. Pour mixture over fruit. Cover, and refrigerate for 1 hour, stirring occasionally. Garnish with mint, if desired.

Grilled Shrimp Cocktail with Roasted Cocktail Sauce
Makes 6 servings

36 large fresh shrimp, peeled and deveined (tails on)
3 tablespoons olive oil
1½ teaspoons seasoned salt
1 teaspoon garlic powder
½ teaspoon ground black pepper
Roasted Tomato Cocktail Sauce (recipe follows)

1. Spray grill rack with nonflammable cooking spray. Preheat grill to medium-high heat (350° to 400°).

2. In a large bowl, combine shrimp, olive oil, seasoned salt, garlic powder, and pepper. Grill for 1 to 2 minutes per side. Serve with Roasted Tomato Cocktail Sauce.

ROASTED TOMATO COCKTAIL SAUCE
Makes about 3½ cups

3 pints grape tomatoes

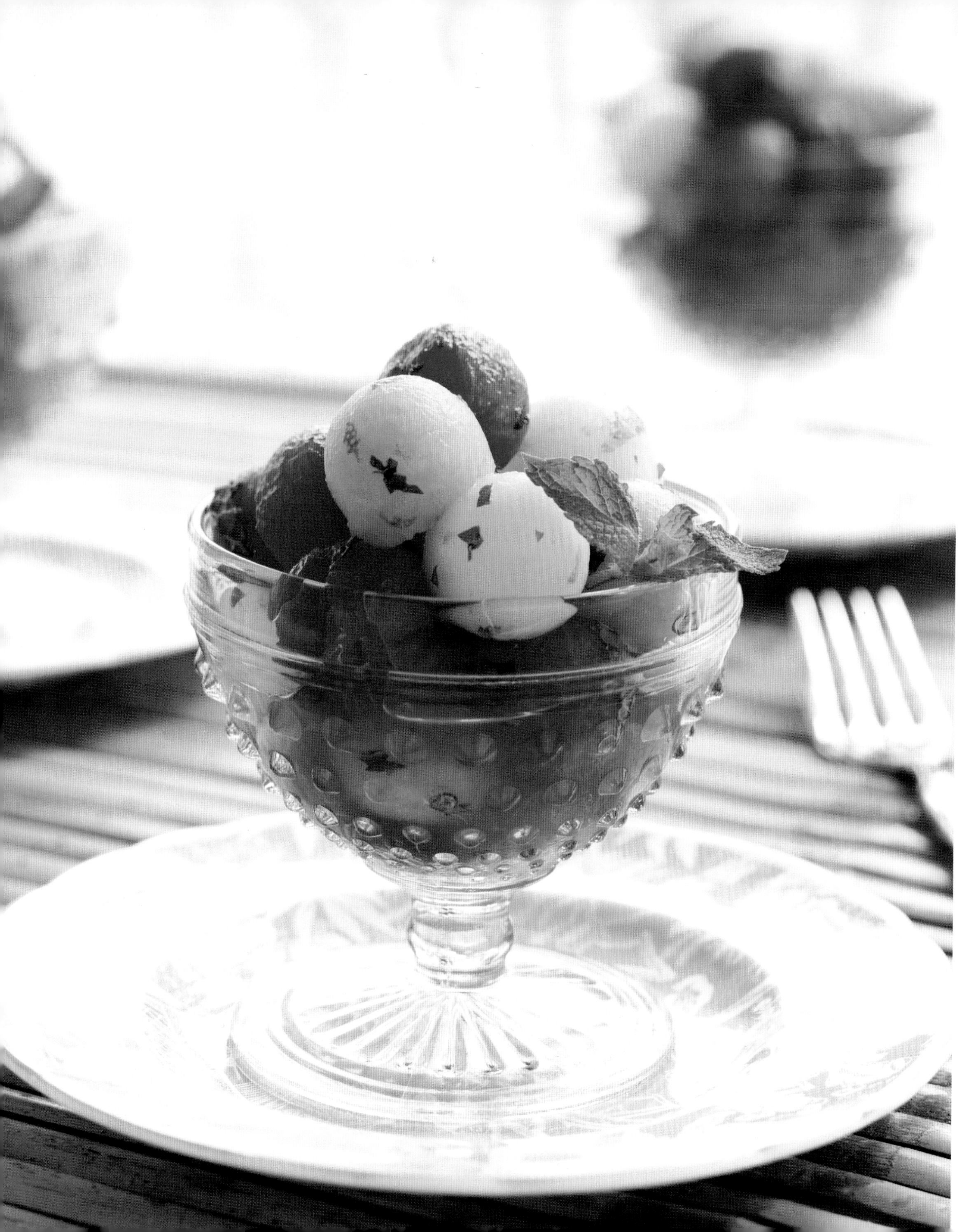

Coconut Cake

Makes 1 (9-inch) cake

- 2¼ cups butter, softened
- 3 cups sugar
- 6 large eggs
- 2 teaspoons coconut extract
- ½ teaspoon vanilla extract
- 3¾ cups all-purpose flour
- 2½ teaspoons baking powder
- ½ teaspoon salt
- 1½ cups whole buttermilk
  Coconut Icing (recipe follows)
- 1 (14-ounce) bag sweetened flaked coconut

1. Preheat oven to 350°. Spray 3 (9-inch) round cake pans with baking spray with flour. Line bottoms of pans with parchment paper, and spray again.

2. In a medium bowl, beat butter and sugar with a mixer at medium speed until fluffy. Add eggs, one at a time, beating well after each addition. Beat in coconut extract and vanilla.

3. In a medium bowl, combine flour, baking powder, and salt. Gradually add flour mixture to butter mixture alternately with buttermilk, beginning and ending with flour mixture. Spoon batter into prepared pans. Bake for 30 to 35 minutes or until a wooden pick inserted in center comes out clean. Let cool in pans for 10 minutes. Remove from pans, and let cool completely on wire racks.

4. Place one cake layer on a serving plate; spread 1½ cups Coconut Icing over layer. Sprinkle with 1 cup coconut. Repeat procedure once. Top with remaining cake layer. Spread remaining Coconut Icing on top and sides of cake. Immediately press remaining coconut onto top and sides of cake. Refrigerate for 1 hour before serving.

COCONUT ICING
Makes about 6 cups

- 2 (8-ounce) packages cream cheese, softened
- 1 cup butter, softened
- 7 cups confectioners' sugar
- 2 teaspoons coconut extract

1. In a large bowl, beat cream cheese and butter with a mixer at medium speed until creamy. Gradually beat in confectioners' sugar until smooth. Beat in coconut extract.

Taste of Summer

Turn a dinner on the dock into a midsummer night's dream come true with easy-breezy recipes and entertaining ideas.

Cast cares away with a date night on the dock that is the epitome of casual chic. Taking cues from the water, cool shades of aqua and indigo bring serenity to the scene, while warmer hues inspired by the setting sun lend a hint of summer fun. Rope and rafia add nautical notes to the décor, and a retro-style mp3 player sets the mood with music. DIY ideas abound in the the form of birch log votive holders to a giant-size version of Jenga. Homemade citronella candles keep bugs at bay and lend a romantic glow—aided by lanterns and string lights. Serve apps on a pallet-style picnic area, then enjoy dinner at a table for two. After dessert, take the canoe out, or simply sit and watch the sky trade the sun for the moon and stars.

Strawberry Basil Gimlet
Makes 2 servings

½   cup water
½   cup sugar
2   strawberries
3   to 4 basil leaves
3   ounces vodka
¼   cup lime juice
Garnish: basil leaves, strawberries

1. In a small saucepan, combine water and sugar over medium-high heat; stir until sugar dissolves. Remove from heat, and let cool completely.

2. In a shaker or 2-cup liquid-measuring cup, combine strawberries, basil leaves, vodka, and lime juice. Using a muddler or the back of a spoon, gently press strawberries and basil to release flavor. Stir in sugar mixture. Strain, and serve over ice. Garnish with basil leaves and strawberries, if desired.

Watermelon Pizza
Makes 2 servings

2   tablespoons balsamic vinegar
1   (1-inch-thick) round slice watermelon
2   tablespoons crumbled goat cheese
2   slices bacon, cooked and crumbled
1   tablespoon chopped fresh mint

1. In a small saucepan, bring vinegar to a boil. Boil for 2 to 3 minutes or until vinegar is reduced by half. Let cool completely.

2. Top watermelon slice with goat cheese, bacon, and mint. Drizzle with vinegar. Slice into wedges.

menu

Strawberry Basil Gimlet
Watermelon Pizza
Grilled Shrimp Kabobs
Orange Almond Orzo
Vanilla Bourbon
Crème Brûlée

Grilled Shrimp Kabobs
Makes 2 servings

- ¼ cup lemon juice
- 2 garlic cloves, chopped
- 2 tablespoons chopped fresh basil
- 1 teaspoon Dijon mustard
- ¼ cup olive oil
- 1 pound large fresh shrimp, peeled and deveined
- 1 cup grape tomatoes
- 1 cup (1-inch pieces) red onion
- 1 cup (1-inch pieces) zucchini
- Garnish: lemon slices

1. In a small bowl, whisk together lemon juice, garlic, basil, and mustard. In a slow, steady stream, whisk in oil. Pour into a large resealable plastic bag. Add shrimp, tomatoes, red onion, and zucchini. Refrigerate for 2 to 4 hours.

2. Place wooden skewers in enough water to cover; soak for at least 30 minutes.

3. Spray grill rack with nonflammable cooking spray. Preheat grill to medium-high heat (350° to 400°).

4. Drain shrimp mixture, discarding marinade. Thread onion, tomatoes, zucchini, and shrimp onto skewers.

5. Arrange skewers on grill, and grill for 3 to 4 minutes per side or until shrimp are done. Garnish with lemon slices, if desired.

Orange Almond Orzo
Makes 2 servings

- 1½ cups cooked orzo
- ¼ cup slivered almonds
- 1 tablespoon butter
- 1 tablespoon grated orange rind
- 1 tablespoon chopped fresh mint
- 1 tablespoon chopped fresh parsley
- ¼ teaspoon salt
- Garnish: orange wedge

1. In a large bowl, combine orzo, almonds, butter, orange rind, mint, parsley, and salt. Garnish with an orange wedge, if desired.

Vanilla Bourbon Crème Brûlée
Makes 2 servings

- 4 egg yolks
- 2 cups heavy whipping cream
- ¼ cup plus 1 tablespoon sugar, divided
- 2 tablespoons bourbon
- 1 vanilla bean, split lengthwise and seeds scraped and reserved
- ¼ teaspoon salt
- 2 strawberry slices

1. Preheat oven to 325°.

2. In a medium bowl, whisk egg yolks.

3. In a small saucepan, combine cream, ¼ cup sugar, bourbon, reserved vanilla bean seeds, and salt. Bring to a simmer over medium-low heat; do not boil. Slowly add cream mixture to egg yolks, whisking constantly. Skim off any foam on top of custard. Evenly divide custard mixture between 2 (8-ounce) custard cups. Place cups in a 13x9-inch baking dish. Pour enough hot water to come halfway up sides of custard cups. Bake for 1 hour and 10 minutes or until centers are set. Loosely shield with foil if custards begin to brown. Carefully remove custard cups from hot water. Let cool on a wire rack for 1 hour. Cover, and refrigerate for 4 hours to overnight.

4. To serve, place sliced strawberry in center of custard cup. Sprinkle remaining 1 tablespoon sugar over custard. Caramelize sugar using a kitchen torch or place under broiler for 1 to 2 minutes or until sugar is melted.

Lowcountry Cocktail Party

Warm ocean breezes dance through palm fronds as the sunset's glorious color is doubled in the sea's reflection. Summer is the perfect time of year for an evening beach gathering by the boardwalk, complete with refreshing cocktails and seafood appetizers.

Firefly Mint Tea
Makes about 1 gallon

- 3 quarts cold water, divided
- 3 family-size tea bags
- 1 (1-ounce) package fresh mint
- 1 cup sugar
- 1½ cups Firefly sweet tea–flavored vodka
- 1 cup Firefly mint tea–flavored vodka
- 6 tablespoons fresh lemon juice
- Garnish: lemon slices, fresh mint sprigs

1. In a medium saucepan, bring 1 quart water to a boil. Remove from heat, and add tea bags and mint; cover and steep for 5 minutes.

2. Strain tea into a large pitcher, and stir in sugar until dissolved. Add vodkas, lemon juice, and remaining 2 quarts water; stir to mix. Cover and refrigerate. Serve over ice. Garnish with lemon slices and mint, if desired.

Salty Dog
Makes 1 drink

- ¾ cup fresh ruby red grapefruit juice
- ½ ounce fresh lime juice
- 1½ ounces vodka
- Garnish: fresh lime juice, coarse kosher salt, lime slices

1. For garnish, dip rim of highball glass into lime juice, then into kosher salt to coat. Fill a shaker halfway with ice. Add grapefruit juice, lime juice, and vodka. Shake vigorously for 5 to 10 seconds. Strain over ice into prepared glass. Garnish with lime slices, if desired.

Fuzzy Navel
Makes 1 drink

- 6 ounces orange juice
- 4 ounces Firefly peach tea–flavored vodka
- ½ ounce peach schnapps
- ¼ ounce orange liqueur
- Garnish: orange slices, peach slices

1. Fill a shaker halfway with ice. Add orange juice, vodka, peach schnapps, and orange liqueur. Shake vigorously for 5 to 10 seconds. Strain into cocktail glass. Garnish with orange slices and peach slices, if desired.

Charleston Crab Cakes with Tomato Chutney

Makes 2 dozen

- 4 (8-ounce) containers jumbo lump crabmeat, picked
- 1½ cups panko (Japanese bread crumbs)
- ½ cup minced red bell pepper
- ¼ cup minced green onion
- 2 tablespoons chopped fresh parsley
- 4 large eggs
- ¼ cup mayonnaise
- 2 tablespoons Dijon mustard
- 4 teaspoons Old Bay Seasoning
- 1 teaspoon salt
- 6 tablespoons vegetable oil, divided
- Tomato Chutney (recipe follows)
- Garnish: chopped green onion

1. In a large bowl, combine crabmeat, panko, bell pepper, green onion, and parsley.

2. In a small bowl, whisk together eggs, mayonnaise, Dijon, Old Bay, and salt. Add egg mixture to crab mixture, tossing gently to combine. Shape crab mixture into 2-inch patties.

3. In a large nonstick skillet, heat 3 tablespoons oil over medium heat. Add crab cakes, and cook for 3 to 4 minutes per side or until golden brown. Repeat with remaining oil and crab cakes. Drain on paper towels. Top with Tomato Chutney. Garnish with green onion, if desired.

TOMATO CHUTNEY
Makes about 3 cups

- 2 tablespoons olive oil
- ½ cup chopped green onion
- 1 tablespoon minced garlic
- 4 cups seeded chopped tomato
- ¼ cup firmly packed dark brown sugar
- 2 tablespoons balsamic vinegar
- 1½ tablespoons prepared horseradish
- ¾ teaspoon salt
- ½ teaspoon ground black pepper

1. In a large saucepan, heat olive oil over medium heat. Add green onion and garlic; cook for 2 to 3 minutes, stirring frequently. Add tomato; cook for 2 to 3 minutes, stirring frequently. Add brown sugar, vinegar, horseradish, salt, and pepper. Reduce heat to medium-low. Simmer, uncovered, for 15 minutes, stirring occasionally.

Lowcountry Salsa
Makes 24 servings

- 3 cups baby lima beans, blanched
- 3 cups fresh corn kernels
- 3 cups sliced okra
- ¼ cup olive oil, divided
- 1½ teaspoons salt, divided
- ½ teaspoon ground black pepper
- 3 cups seeded chopped tomato
- 1 bunch green onions, chopped
- 2 jalapeño peppers, seeded and minced
- 6 tablespoons white-wine vinegar
- 1 teaspoon garlic powder
- ¼ teaspoon ground red pepper
- Garnish: chopped red bell pepper

1. Preheat oven to 450°. Line a rimmed baking sheet with foil.

2. In a large bowl, combine lima beans, corn, okra, 2 tablespoons olive oil, 1 teaspoon salt, and pepper, tossing to coat. Spread lima bean mixture in an even layer onto prepared pan. Bake for 30 minutes. Let cool in pan for 10 minutes.

3. In a large bowl, combine lima bean mixture, tomato, green onions, jalapeños, remaining 2 tablespoons olive oil, vinegar, garlic powder, remaining ½ teaspoon salt, and red pepper, tossing to combine. Cover, and refrigerate for at least 1 hour. Garnish with red bell pepper, if desired.

Savory Shrimp Boil Cheesecakes
Makes 2 dozen

Crust:
- 2 cups firmly packed round buttery cracker crumbs
- 1 cup finely grated Parmesan cheese
- 6 tablespoons butter, melted
- 1 large egg white

Filling:
- 2 tablespoons olive oil
- ½ cup fresh corn kernels
- ½ cup finely chopped red bell pepper
- ¼ cup finely chopped green onion
- 1 tablespoon minced garlic
- 1 cup finely chopped fresh shrimp
- 1 cup finely chopped smoked sausage
- ½ teaspoon salt
- ½ teaspoon ground red pepper
- 2 (8-ounce) packages cream cheese, softened
- 2 large egg yolks
- Garnish: ground red pepper, chopped fresh parsley

1. Preheat oven to 350°.

2. To prepare crust: In a medium bowl, combine cracker crumbs, Parmesan cheese, melted butter, and egg white, stirring to mix well. Press into bottom and halfway up sides of 2 (12-cup) mini cheesecake pans. Bake for 6 minutes.

3. To prepare filling: In a medium skillet, heat olive oil over medium heat. Add corn, bell pepper, green onion, and garlic; cook for 3 minutes, stirring frequently. Add shrimp, sausage, salt, and red pepper; cook for 2 minutes, stirring frequently. Remove from heat, and let cool for 5 minutes.

4. In a medium bowl, combine cream cheese and egg yolks. Beat with a mixer at medium speed until creamy. Add shrimp mixture to cream cheese mixture, beating to combine. Spoon cream cheese mixture evenly into baked crusts. Bake for 16 to 18 minutes or until set. Garnish with ground red pepper and parsley, if desired.

Fried Oyster Rolls
Makes 12 servings

- 2 cups Wondra flour
- 4 teaspoons Old Bay Seasoning
- 2 teaspoons salt
- 1 teaspoon ground red pepper
- Vegetable oil for frying
- 4 (8-ounce) containers shucked oysters (3 dozen)
- Remoulade (recipe follows)
- 6 hoagie rolls, halved and split
- Shredded green leaf lettuce
- Sliced plum tomatoes

1. In a shallow dish, combine flour, Old Bay, salt, and red pepper.

2. In a large Dutch oven, pour oil to a depth of 4 inches, and heat to 350° over medium heat.

3. Dredge oysters in flour mixture, shaking off excess. Cook for 1 to 2 minutes or until golden brown. Drain on paper towels. Spread Remoulade onto hoagie rolls. Top with fried oysters, lettuce, and tomatoes.

REMOULADE
Makes about 1½ cups

- 1 cup mayonnaise
- 2 tablespoons Creole mustard
- ¼ cup sweet pickle relish
- 2 tablespoons ketchup
- 2 tablespoons chopped fresh parsley
- 1 tablespoon minced capers
- 1 tablespoon minced green onion
- 1 tablespoon hot sauce
- ½ teaspoon garlic powder

1. In a medium bowl, combine mayonnaise, mustard, pickle relish, ketchup, parsley, capers, green onion, hot sauce, and garlic powder, stirring to combine well. Cover, and refrigerate until ready to serve.

Toasted Coconut Shortcakes with Pineapple Mousse
Makes about 1 dozen

- 3 cups all-purpose flour
- ¾ cup plus 1 tablespoon sugar, divided
- 1 tablespoon baking powder
- ¾ cup cold butter, cut into pieces
- 1 cup toasted coconut
- 1½ cups plus 2 tablespoons heavy whipping cream, divided
- 1 teaspoon coconut extract
- Pineapple Mousse (recipe follows)
- Garnish: toasted coconut, white chocolate curls, fresh strawberries

1. Preheat oven to 400°. Line a baking sheet with parchment paper; set aside.

2. In a medium bowl, combine flour, ¾ cup sugar, and baking powder, stirring to mix well. Using a pastry blender, cut butter into flour mixture until crumbly. Stir in coconut.

3. In a 2-cup measuring cup, combine 1½ cups cream and coconut extract. Add cream mixture to flour mixture, and stir until dough is just combined.

4. On a lightly floured surface, roll dough to 1-inch thickness. Using a 2½-inch round cutter, cut dough, and place on prepared pan, 2 inches apart. Brush tops with remaining 2 tablespoons cream, and sprinkle with remaining 1 tablespoon sugar. Bake for 15 to 17 minutes or until lightly browned. Let cool on pan for 10 minutes. Serve with Pineapple Mousse. Garnish with toasted coconut, white chocolate curls, and fresh strawberries, if desired.

PINEAPPLE MOUSSE
Makes 12 servings

- 1 (3.4-ounce) box vanilla-flavored instant pudding mix
- 1 (20-ounce) can crushed pineapple, undrained
- 1¾ cups heavy whipping cream
- 2 tablespoons pineapple-flavored rum

1. In a medium bowl, combine pudding mix and pineapple; let stand for 5 minutes. Add cream and rum. Beat with a mixer at medium-high speed until stiff peaks form.

Supper Club Fiesta

Bursting with color and bold Tex-Mex flavor, this menu featuring make-ahead dishes is just right for Cinco de Mayo or your next family-style dinner party.

A supper club is a great way to set aside regular time with friends. Keep it manageable by rotating houses, and for extra fun, try different themes for settings and menus. This fiesta-style setup works for a few or a crowd—you can mix-and-match plates and linens to create a lively scene. And because about half the menu can be made in advance, it takes day-of dinner prep from oy to olé!

Garnish: chopped green onion
Herbed Pita Chips (recipe follows)

1. Preheat oven to 400°.

2. In a large saucepan, sauté bacon over medium-high heat for 3 to 4 minutes or until lightly browned. Add onion and garlic; sauté for 3 to 4 minutes or until translucent. Add corn, and sauté for 2 to 3 minutes or until hot. Remove from heat.

3. In a large bowl, combine corn mixture, Monterey Jack cheese, 1 cup Parmesan cheese, mayonnaise, and cream cheese. Spread into a 13x9-inch baking dish. Sprinkle remaining ½ cup Parmesan cheese evenly over corn mixture, and bake for 20 to 25 minutes or until golden brown and bubbly. Garnish with chopped green onion, if desired. Serve with Herbed Pita Chips.

Note: Frozen corn may be substituted for fresh. Dip can be made a day in advance and stored, covered, in the refrigerator. Set out an hour before baking.

HERBED PITA CHIPS
Makes 8 to 10 servings

- 2   teaspoons dried thyme
- 2   teaspoons dried oregano
- 4   (6-inch) pita bread rounds
- ½   cup olive oil

1. Preheat oven to 375°. Line a baking sheet with parchment paper.

2. In a small bowl, combine thyme and oregano.

3. Cut each pita round into 8 triangles. Cut each triangle in half, lengthwise, so that there are 64 thin triangles. Arrange in a single layer on prepared pan. Brush triangles with olive oil, and sprinkle with herb mixture. Bake for 10 to 12 minutes or until lightly browned. Repeat with remaining pita.

Frozen Watermelon Margarita
Makes 8 servings

- 8   cups frozen cubed watermelon, divided
- 2   (12-ounce) cans frozen limeade concentrate, divided
- 2   cups tequila, divided
- 1   cup orange liqueur, divided
- 2   tablespoons chopped jalapeño, divided

Garnish: salt, small jalapeño or serrano peppers

1. In the container of a blender, combine 4 cups watermelon, 1 can frozen limeade concentrate, 1 cup tequila, ½ cup liqueur, and 1 tablespoon jalapeño. (Blender will be full.) Process until smooth. Pour into a large resealable plastic bag. Freeze until ready to serve. Repeat with remaining ingredients. Pour into another large resealable plastic bag. Garnish glasses with salt and jalapeño or serrano pepper, if desired.

Note: The margaritas can be made a few days in advance.

Corn and Bacon Dip
Makes 8 to 10 servings

- 3   bacon strips, diced
- ¼   cup diced onion
- 2   garlic cloves, minced
- 6   cups fresh corn
- 2   cups Monterey Jack cheese
- 1½   cups Parmesan cheese, divided
- 1   cup mayonnaise
- 1   (8-ounce) package cream cheese, softened

menu

Frozen Watermelon
Margarita

Corn and Bacon Dip

Pork and Lime Kabobs

Spicy Black Beans

Jicama Slaw

Churros with Dulce de Leche

Blueberry Granita

Pork and Lime Kabobs

Makes 8 servings

- 1   cup soy sauce
- ½   cup lime juice
- ½   cup balsamic vinegar
- ½   cup olive oil
- ¼   teaspoon ground red pepper

- 1   (3-pound) pork tenderloin, cut into 1½-inch pieces
- 1   medium red onion, cut into 1-inch pieces
- 8   button mushrooms, cut in half
- 16 lime slices
- Garnish: lime slices

1. In a large bowl, whisk together soy sauce, lime juice, vinegar, olive oil, and red pepper. Place pork, onion, and mushrooms in a large resealable plastic bag; add soy sauce mixture. Seal bag, and refrigerate for 1 hour or up to 4 hours.

2. In a shallow dish, place wooden skewers in enough water to cover; soak for 30 minutes.

3. Spray grill rack with nonflammable

cooking spray. Preheat grill to medium-high heat (350° to 400°).

4. Drain pork mixture, discarding marinade. Thread pork, onion, mushrooms, and lime slices onto skewers. Arrange skewers on grill, and grill for 4 to 5 minutes per side or until pork is done. Garnish with lime slices, if desired.

Spicy Black Beans
Makes 8 servings

  1   (1-pound) package dried black beans
  1   tablespoon olive oil
  1   cup diced sweet onion
  4   garlic cloves, chopped
  1   tablespoon cumin
  1   tablespoon salt
  ½   teaspoon ground red pepper
  Garnish: cilantro leaves

1. Soak beans according to package directions. Drain and set aside.

2. In a large saucepan, heat olive oil over medium-high heat until hot. Add onion and garlic, and sauté for 2 to 3 minutes or until translucent. Stir in cumin, salt, and pepper. Add beans and water to cover beans. Bring to a boil. Reduce heat to low, cover, and cook for 1½ hours or until beans are tender. Garnish with cilantro leaves, if desired.

Jicama Slaw
Makes 8 servings

  ¼   cup rice vinegar
  ¼   cup lime juice
  ½   cup olive oil
  7   cups packed thinly sliced napa cabbage
  2   cups peeled and julienned jicama
  2   cups chopped pineapple
  ½   cup chopped fresh cilantro

1. In a small bowl, whisk together vinegar and lime juice. Whisking constantly, slowly drizzle in olive oil.

2. In a large bowl, combine cabbage, jicama, pineapple, and cilantro. To serve, toss with vinaigrette. Serve immediately.

DULCE DE LECHE
Makes 8 servings

- 4 **cups whole milk**
- 1 **cup sugar**
- 1 **vanilla bean, split and scraped**
- ¼ **teaspoon salt**
- ½ **teaspoon baking soda**

1. In a medium saucepan, combine milk, sugar, vanilla bean, and salt over medium-high heat. Bring to a boil. Reduce heat to medium-low, and simmer until sugar dissolves, stirring occasionally. Reduce heat to low, and add baking soda. Simmer for 2½ hours or until sauce is light brown and thickened, stirring occasionally. Strain through a fine-mesh strainer into a bowl. Serve with Churros.

Blueberry Granita
Makes 8 servings

- 3 **cups water**
- 3 **cups sugar**
- 1 **tablespoon grated orange zest**
- 8 **cups fresh blueberries, divided**
- **Garnish: mint leaves**

1. In a medium saucepan, combine water and sugar. Bring to a boil over medium-high heat; reduce heat and simmer, stirring until sugar dissolves. Remove from heat, and let cool completely.

2. In the container of a blender, combine 1½ cups sugar mixture, orange zest, and 4 cups blueberries; process until smooth. Pour into a 13x9-inch baking pan. Repeat with remaining 1½ cups sugar mixture and 4 cups blueberries. Pour into baking pan, and combine with a whisk. Cover, and freeze for at least 8 hours or until firm. Before serving, scrape mixture with a fork until fluffy. Garnish with mint leaves, if desired.

Note: Freeze serving dishes before filling with granita because it melts quickly. Granita can be made a day in advance.

Churros with Dulce de Leche
Makes 8 servings

- 1 **cup water**
- ½ **cup butter**
- ¼ **teaspoon salt**
- 1 **cup all-purpose flour**
- 3 **large eggs, beaten**
- ¼ **cup sugar**
- ½ **teaspoon ground cinnamon**
- **Vegetable oil**
- **Dulce de Leche (recipe follows)**

1. In a medium saucepan, combine water, butter, and salt over medium-high heat. Bring to a boil. Reduce heat to low, and add flour, stirring constantly, until dough forms a ball. Remove from heat, and stir in eggs.

2. Spoon dough into a pastry bag fitted with a large star tip.

3. In a small bowl, combine sugar and cinnamon. Sprinkle onto a plate.

4. In a Dutch oven or deep fryer, pour oil to a depth of 3 inches. Heat oil over medium heat to 360°. On another plate, pipe dough in 3- to 4-inch-long logs. Fry churros, in batches, for 2 to 3 minutes per side or until golden brown. Carefully remove, and place on paper-towel-lined plate to drain. When cool enough to handle, roll in sugar mixture. Serve with Dulce de Leche.

Note: If dough is too soft to handle, refrigerate for 1 hour before frying. Or make it the night before, and let chill. Remove from refrigerator 1 hour before frying.

Enchanted Evening

As the sunset paints the sky the brilliant shades of fall leaves, gather friends for an elegant outdoor meal served in dazzling surroundings.

Something as simple as adding bright hypericum berries and Spanish moss to an ivy-covered column or stringing café lights from tree to tree enhances the romance of this setting. To play up the elegance, add golden accents, such as gilded pumpkins, amber glasses, and leaf-patterned china. From soup to sweets, this dressed-up dinner will shine as brightly as the harvest moon that holds sway over this sublime autumn soirée.

The shimmer of candlelight casts a romantic aura over this autumnal gathering in the garden. In lieu of a table runner, line up cotton-lace doilies, and top them with a medley of glass bottles filled with tapers. Intersperse stems of blush roses, dusty miller, and hypericum berries among the bottles. Monogrammed silver napkin rings and goblets etched in a gold filigree pattern add a polished note to the setting.

Arugula Salad with Sautéed Mushrooms, Prosciutto, and Truffle Dressing

Makes 8 servings

¼ cup olive oil, divided
2 (8-ounce) containers sliced baby portobello mushrooms
1 tablespoon minced garlic
¼ teaspoon salt
¼ teaspoon ground black pepper
1 (3.53-ounce) package prosciutto, chopped
2 (4-ounce) bags arugula

Truffle Dressing (recipe follows)
Garnish: shaved Parmesan cheese

1. In a large skillet, heat 2 tablespoons olive oil over medium heat. Add mushrooms, garlic, salt, and pepper; cook for 10 minutes, stirring occasionally, until lightly browned. Remove and set aside.

2. Heat remaining 2 tablespoons olive oil over medium heat. Add prosciutto; cook for 15 to 20 minutes, stirring frequently, until lightly browned. Divide arugula, mushrooms, and prosciutto among 8 salad plates. Drizzle with Truffle Dressing. Garnish with shaved Parmesan, if desired.

TRUFFLE DRESSING
Makes 2½ cups

1 cup mayonnaise
1 cup sour cream
½ cup white truffle oil
¼ cup water
2 tablespoons Champagne vinegar
¼ teaspoon salt
¼ teaspoon ground black pepper

1. In the container of a blender, combine mayonnaise, sour cream, truffle oil, water, vinegar, salt, and pepper. Process until well combined.

menu

Arugula Salad with Sautéed Mushrooms, Prosciutto, and Truffle Dressing

Roasted Squash Soup

Pork Madeira with Parmesan Polenta

Roasted Broccolini

Pumpkin Trifles

2 tablespoons olive oil over medium heat. Add onion, bay leaves, and garlic; cook for 10 minutes, stirring frequently. Add cooked squash and chicken broth. Reduce heat to low; cover, and simmer for 30 minutes. Remove and discard bay leaves. Let cool for 10 minutes.

4. In the container of a blender, purée squash mixture in batches.

5. Return to Dutch oven over medium-low heat. Add cheese, cream, sour cream, sugar, poultry seasoning, garlic powder, remaining ½ teaspoon pepper, and remaining ¼ teaspoon salt, whisking to combine. Cook for 5 minutes, stirring constantly, until cheese melts. Serve with Seasoned Croutons.

SEASONED CROUTONS
Makes 8 cups

- ½ cup butter, melted
- 1 teaspoon poultry seasoning
- ½ teaspoon garlic salt
- 1 (8.5-ounce) French baguette, cut into 1-inch pieces

1. Preheat oven to 400°. Line a rimmed baking sheet with foil.

2. In a large bowl, combine melted butter, poultry seasoning, and garlic salt. Add bread pieces, tossing to coat. Spread in an even layer on prepared pan. Bake for 10 minutes or until lightly browned.

Roasted Squash Soup
Makes 5 quarts

- 5 pounds yellow squash, cut into ½-inch pieces
- ¼ cup olive oil, divided
- 1¼ teaspoons salt, divided
- 1 teaspoon ground black pepper, divided
- 1 yellow onion, chopped
- 3 bay leaves
- 1 tablespoon minced garlic
- 3 quarts chicken broth
- 4 cups shredded sharp Cheddar cheese
- 1 cup heavy whipping cream
- ½ cup sour cream
- 1 teaspoon sugar
- 1 teaspoon poultry seasoning
- ½ teaspoon garlic powder
- Seasoned Croutons (recipe follows)

1. Preheat oven to 400°. Line a rimmed baking sheet with heavy-duty foil.

2. In a large bowl, combine squash, 2 tablespoons olive oil, 1 teaspoon salt, and ½ teaspoon pepper, tossing to coat. Spread squash in an even layer onto prepared pan. Bake for 1 hour.

3. In a large Dutch oven, heat remaining

Pork Madeira with Parmesan Polenta
Makes 8 servings

- 1 cup all-purpose flour
- 2 teaspoons salt
- 1 teaspoon ground black pepper
- 10 tablespoons olive oil, divided
- 2 (1-pound) pork tenderloins, cut into ½-inch-thick pieces

- 2 large yellow onions, thinly sliced
- 1 tablespoon minced garlic
- 3 tablespoons all-purpose flour
- 3 cups beef broth
- 2 tablespoons Worcestershire sauce
- ¾ teaspoon salt
- ¼ teaspoon ground black pepper
- 1 cup Madeira
- 2 tablespoons chopped fresh thyme
  Parmesan Polenta (recipe follows)
  Garnish: chopped fresh thyme

1. In a shallow dish, combine flour, salt, and pepper.

2. In a large nonstick skillet, heat 2 tablespoons olive oil over medium-high heat. Dredge pork in flour mixture, shaking to remove excess. Cook pork, in batches, for 2 minutes per side, until lightly browned, wiping skillet clean between batches. Repeat with remaining olive oil and pork, reserving 2 tablespoons olive oil. Set pork aside.

3. In skillet, heat reserved 2 tablespoons olive oil over medium heat. Add onions and garlic; cook for 20 minutes, stirring frequently. Add flour; cook for 2 minutes, stirring constantly. Gradually add beef broth, Worcestershire sauce, salt, and pepper. Bring to a simmer; cook for 10 minutes. Add Madeira and thyme, stirring to combine well. Add pork to skillet; cook for 2 minutes or until pork is heated through. Serve over Parmesan Polenta. Garnish with chopped fresh thyme, if desired.

PARMESAN POLENTA
Makes 8 servings

- 8 cups whole milk
- 1¾ teaspoons salt
- ½ teaspoon ground black pepper
- 1¾ cups stone-ground yellow cornmeal
- 1½ cups finely grated Parmigiano-Reggiano cheese
- ¼ cup butter

1. In a large Dutch oven, combine milk, salt, and pepper over medium heat. Bring

to a simmer; do not boil. Gradually add cornmeal, whisking to combine. Reduce heat to low; cover, and cook for 30 minutes, stirring occasionally. Add cheese and butter, stirring until cheese is melted.

Roasted Broccolini
Makes 8 servings

- ½ cup teriyaki sauce
- ½ cup water
- 2 tablespoons firmly packed dark brown sugar
- 2 teaspoons garlic powder
- ½ cup olive oil

- 4 bunches broccolini, tough stems removed
- 1 tablespoon minced dried onion

1. Preheat oven to 400°. Line a rimmed baking sheet with foil.

2. In a large bowl, combine teriyaki sauce, water, brown sugar, and garlic powder, whisking until sugar dissolves. Gradually add olive oil, whisking to combine well. Add broccolini, tossing to coat. Spread broccolini in an even layer into prepared pan; pour teriyaki mixture over top. Sprinkle with minced dried onion. Bake for 15 to 20 minutes or until tender.

*"In the entire circle
of the year there are no
days so delightful as
those of a fine October...."*
—Alexander Smith

Pumpkin Trifles
Makes 8 servings

　1　cup canned pumpkin
　1　(8-ounce) container frozen
　　　nondairy whipped topping, thawed
　　　and divided
　1　cup confectioners' sugar, divided
1½　teaspoons pumpkin pie spice
　½　teaspoon ground cinnamon
　¼　teaspoon salt
　1　(8-ounce) package cream cheese,
　　　softened
　2　teaspoons vanilla extract
　1　cup gingersnap cookie crumbs
　　　Garnish: whipped cream, pumpkin pie
　　　　spice, gingersnaps

1. In a medium bowl, combine pumpkin,
½ container whipped topping, ½ cup
confectioners' sugar, pumpkin pie spice,
cinnamon, and salt. Beat with a mixer at
medium speed until well combined;
set aside.

2. In a medium bowl, combine cream
cheese, remaining ½ container whipped
topping, remaining ½ cup confectioners'
sugar, and vanilla extract. Beat with a
mixer at medium speed until smooth.

3. In small glasses, layer cream cheese
mixture, gingersnap cookie crumbs, and
pumpkin mixture. Garnish with whipped
cream, pumpkin pie spice, and
gingersnaps, if desired.

ENTERTAINING COOKBOOK
VOL. 2

Best
RECIPES

We've assembled more than 65 of our favorite recipes to help design both special occasion menus and easy family meals.

1
Scrumptious
APPETIZERS AND BEVERAGES

Make a delicious first impression by welcoming guests with a tantalizing array of starters. Savory hors d'oeuvres paired with refreshing sippers allow partygoers to mix and mingle while whetting their appetites for the dinner to come—or serve several of these scrumptious appetizers together to create a meal all on their own.

Fried Pickled Okra
Makes 16 to 20 servings

Vegetable oil for frying
2 cups yellow self-rising cornmeal mix
1 cup all-purpose flour
1 teaspoon garlic powder
1 teaspoon ground red pepper
½ teaspoon seasoned salt
½ teaspoon ground black pepper
4 (16-ounce) jars spicy pickled okra*, halved
   lengthwise, ½ cup juice reserved
1 large egg
Horseradish Dipping Sauce (recipe follows)

1. In a large skillet, pour oil to a depth of 1½ inches. Heat oil over medium heat to 350°.

2. In a shallow dish, combine cornmeal mix, flour, garlic powder, red pepper, seasoned salt, and black pepper.

3. In a separate shallow dish, combine reserved pickled okra juice and egg, whisking to combine. Dip pickled okra into egg mixture, allowing excess to drain. Coat pickled okra in cornmeal mixture. Fry in batches for 1 to 2 minutes per batch or until golden brown. Drain on paper towels. Serve with Horseradish Dipping Sauce.

We used Wickles Wicked Okra.

HORSERADISH DIPPING SAUCE
Makes about 2 cups

1 (16-ounce) container sour cream
½ cup mayonnaise
¼ cup prepared horseradish
1 teaspoon garlic powder
½ teaspoon seasoned salt
½ teaspoon ground black pepper
¼ teaspoon ground red pepper

1. In a medium bowl, combine sour cream, mayonnaise, horseradish, garlic powder, seasoned salt, black pepper, and red pepper, stirring to combine well.

Pimiento Cheese–Stuffed Tomatoes

Makes 10 to 15 servings

- 1 (8-ounce) block sharp Cheddar cheese, shredded
- 1 (8-ounce) block Monterey Jack cheese, shredded
- 2 (4-ounce) jars diced pimientos, drained
- 1¼ cups mayonnaise
- ½ cup chopped toasted pecans
- 2 tablespoons dill pickle relish
- 1 teaspoon sugar
- ½ teaspoon garlic powder
- ½ teaspoon ground black pepper
- 2 (1-pound) containers Campari tomatoes

1. In a medium bowl, combine cheeses, pimientos, mayonnaise, pecans, dill pickle relish, sugar, garlic powder, and pepper, stirring to combine well.

2. Using a serrated knife, cut a thin slice off bottoms of tomatoes to create a level base. Cut tops from tomatoes. Using a melon baller, remove pulp, leaving shells intact. Turn tomatoes upside down on paper towels to drain for 10 minutes. To serve, spoon pimiento cheese into tomato shells.

Bacon-Topped Deviled Eggs
Makes 3 dozen

18 large eggs
½ cup mayonnaise
6 tablespoons sweet pickle relish
1 tablespoon dill pickle juice
2 teaspoons yellow mustard
½ teaspoon ground black pepper
Garnish: cooked crumbled bacon

1. Place eggs in a large saucepan with enough cold water to cover; cook over high heat until water begins to boil.

2. Reduce heat to medium; simmer eggs for 10 minutes.

3. Remove from heat; drain eggs, and rinse with cold water. Peel eggs, discarding shells. Halve eggs lengthwise.

4. Remove yolks, and place in a small bowl. Mash yolks with a fork until crumbly. Add mayonnaise, sweet pickle relish, dill pickle juice, mustard, and pepper, stirring until well combined. Spoon egg yolk mixture evenly into egg whites. Garnish with bacon, if desired.

BLT Roll-Ups

Makes about 6 dozen

- 4 (8-ounce) packages cream cheese, softened
- 1 pound bacon, cooked and crumbled
- 2 cups finely shredded Cheddar cheese
- 1½ cups seeded chopped tomatoes
- 1½ cups chopped green leaf lettuce
- 1 teaspoon garlic powder
- 6 large flour tortillas

1. In a large bowl, combine cream cheese, bacon, Cheddar cheese, tomatoes, lettuce, and garlic powder. Beat with a mixer at medium speed until well combined. Spread about 1 cup filling evenly onto tortillas to the edge. Roll up, and wrap tightly in plastic wrap. Refrigerate for 2 hours to overnight.

2. Remove plastic wrap, and cut into ½-inch-thick slices.

"Cooking is like love, it should be entered into with abandon or not at all." —Harriet van Horne

Spicy Meatballs
Makes 4 dozen

- 2 pounds ground chuck
- 2 pounds spicy Italian sausage, casings removed
- 2 large eggs, lightly beaten
- 1 large yellow onion, chopped
- 1 tablespoon minced garlic
- 1 cup panko (Japanese bread crumbs)
- 2 teaspoons salt
- 2 teaspoons garlic powder
- ½ teaspoon ground black pepper
- Barbecue Sauce (recipe follows)

1. In a large bowl, combine ground chuck, sausage, eggs, onion, garlic, panko, salt, garlic powder, and pepper. Using hands, mix and shape meat mixture into 2-inch balls. Place meatballs in a slow cooker. Pour Barbecue Sauce over meatballs. Cover, and cook on High for 4 hours.

BARBECUE SAUCE
Makes about 4 cups

- 2 cups water
- 2 cups ketchup
- 1¼ cups distilled white vinegar
- 6 tablespoons firmly packed dark brown sugar
- 2 tablespoons paprika
- 2 tablespoons Worcestershire sauce
- 1 teaspoon salt
- ½ teaspoon ground black pepper
- ½ teaspoon ground red pepper (optional)

1. In a medium bowl, whisk together water, ketchup, vinegar, brown sugar, paprika, Worcestershire sauce, salt, black pepper, and red pepper (if desired).

Southern-Style Lemony Iced Tea

Makes 6 to 8 servings

6   small tea bags
½   cup sugar
1   gallon boiling water
1   (6-ounce) can frozen lemonade concentrate

1. In a plastic or heat-resistant gallon pitcher, place tea bags and sugar. Fill with boiling water, and let steep for 2 hours.

2. Remove tea bags. Stir in lemonade concentrate, and refrigerate until cool. Serve over ice.

Almond Butter Smoothies

Makes 4 to 6 servings

2   cups vanilla low-fat frozen yogurt
1   cup almond milk
½   cup almond butter
2   tablespoons honey
1   vanilla bean, split and scraped, seeds reserved

1. In the container of a blender, combine yogurt, almond milk, almond butter, honey, and vanilla bean seeds. Process until well combined. Serve immediately.

Strawberry Party Punch
Makes 40 (8-ounce) servings

1½ quarts water, divided
¾ cup sugar
3 (10-ounce) packages frozen strawberries in syrup, slightly thawed
2 (12-ounce) cans frozen lemonade concentrate
2 (46-ounce) cans pineapple juice
2 (2-liter) bottles ginger ale

1. In a small saucepan, combine 1½ cups water and sugar. Warm over medium heat on stove top, stirring often, until sugar is dissolved. Remove from heat, and set aside to let cool.

2. In a blender, purée strawberries in 3 batches, adding 1½ cups water to each batch before processing.

3. In a 6- to 8-quart container, combine puréed strawberries, sugar mixture, lemonade concentrate, and pineapple juice; stir. Divide mixture between 2 freezer-safe containers. Freeze overnight. Prior to serving, thaw for 2 to 4 hours or until desired slushy consistency is reached. In a 6-quart punch bowl, combine 1 container fruit mixture and 1 bottle ginger ale.

Lavender-Citrus Champagne
Makes 12 servings

1 cup water
½ cup sugar
2 tablespoons chopped fresh lavender or 1 tablespoon dried lavender
4½ cups grapefruit juice
2 (750-ml) bottles brut Champagne or sparkling wine, chilled

1. In a small saucepan, combine water, sugar, and lavender; bring to a boil. Boil until sugar is dissolved, about 1 minute. Let cool completely. Strain sugar syrup through a fine-mesh sieve over a bowl; discard lavender.

2. In a pitcher, combine lavender syrup, juice, and Champagne. Serve over ice. Serve immediately.

Hot Dulce de Leche
Makes 2 quarts

- 4 cups whole milk
- 2 cups heavy whipping cream
- 1 (12-ounce) can evaporated milk
- 1 (13.4-ounce) can dulce de leche*
- ¼ cup firmly packed light brown sugar
- Garnish: whipped cream, caramel topping

1. In a medium Dutch oven, combine milk, cream, and evaporated milk over medium heat. Bring to a simmer; do not boil. Add dulce de leche and brown sugar, stirring until dissolved. Garnish with whipped cream and caramel topping, if desired.

We used Nestlé La Lechera Dulce de Leche.

Chai Egg Nog Punch
Makes about 1 gallon

- 12 cups whole milk
- 1½ cups sugar
- 8 large eggs, lightly beaten
- 8 large egg yolks, lightly beaten
- 2 cups bourbon
- 2 tablespoons vanilla extract
- 1 teaspoon ground cinnamon
- 1 teaspoon ground nutmeg
- 1 teaspoon ground ginger
- 1 teaspoon ground cardamom
- 1 teaspoon ground cloves
- ½ teaspoon salt
- Garnish: whipped cream, ground nutmeg

1. In a large Dutch oven, combine milk, sugar, eggs, and egg yolks over medium-low heat, whisking until smooth. Cook for 25 to 30 minutes, stirring constantly, until mixture coats the back of a spoon. Remove from heat.

2. Strain milk mixture through a fine-mesh strainer into a 1-gallon pitcher. Stir in bourbon, vanilla, cinnamon, nutmeg, ginger, cardamom, cloves, and salt. Cover, and refrigerate for at least 4 hours or up to 2 days. Garnish with whipped cream and nutmeg, if desired.

Ginger Iced Tea
Makes about 1 gallon

2½ quarts cold water, divided
3 family-size tea bags
Ginger Syrup (recipe follows)
Garnish: cinnamon sticks, lemon curls

1. In a medium saucepan, bring 1 quart water to a boil; remove from heat. Add tea bags; cover, and steep for 5 minutes. Strain tea into a large pitcher. Add Ginger Syrup and remaining 1½ quarts water, stirring to mix well. Serve over ice. Garnish with cinnamon sticks and lemon curls, if desired.

GINGER SYRUP
Makes about 2½ cups

2 cups sugar
2 cups water
3 cinnamon sticks
2 tablespoons freshly grated ginger

1. In a medium saucepan, combine sugar and water over medium-high heat, stirring until sugar dissolves. Add cinnamon sticks and ginger. Bring to a boil, reduce heat to medium-low, and simmer for 15 minutes. Cover, and steep for 10 minutes. Strain sugar-syrup mixture, discarding solids; let cool completely.

Homemade Spiced Apple Cider
Makes about 2½ quarts

5 medium Gala apples, cored and quartered
1 medium Granny Smith apple, cored and quartered
3 quarts water
¾ to 1 cup firmly packed dark brown sugar*
½ teaspoon ground cinnamon
½ teaspoon ground allspice
¼ teaspoon ground cloves
¼ teaspoon ground cardamom

1. In a Dutch oven, combine apples, water, brown sugar, cinnamon, allspice, cloves, and cardamom over medium-high heat. Bring to a boil, reduce heat to medium, and

cook, uncovered, stirring occasionally, for 1 hour. Cover pot, reduce heat to medium-low, and simmer for 2 hours. Remove from heat, and let cool completely.

2. Using the back of a spoon, press apple mixture through a fine-mesh sieve into a large pitcher, discarding solids. Reheat to serve.

*The amount of sugar needed may vary, depending on the sweetness of the apples.

2

Enticing BREADS

Whether it's a pan of gussied-up cornbread or a tangy lemon loaf flecked with poppy seeds, bread is an oh-so delectable component of any meal. These favorites pair as nicely with a casual family supper as they do with a soirée for friends.

1. Preheat oven to 350°. Spray 8 (6x3-inch) mini loaf pans with baking spray with flour. Place on a large rimmed baking sheet.

2. In a large bowl, combine butter and sugar. Beat with a mixer at medium speed until fluffy. Add eggs, one at a time, beating well after each addition.

3. In a small bowl, combine flour, baking powder, baking soda, and salt. Gradually add flour mixture to butter mixture alternately with milk, beginning and ending with flour mixture. Beat in sour cream, poppy seeds, lemon zest, and lemon extract. Spoon batter into prepared pans. Bake for 30 to 35 minutes or until a wooden pick inserted in center comes out clean. Let cool in pans for 10 minutes. Remove from pans, and let cool completely on wire racks.

4. In a small bowl, combine confectioners' sugar and lemon juice, whisking until smooth. Drizzle confectioners' sugar mixture on top of loaves. Let stand for 30 minutes or until set.

Cheesy Cornmeal Rolls
Makes 1 dozen

¼	cup butter, softened
2	cups all-purpose flour
⅔	cup yellow cornmeal
2	tablespoons sugar
1½	teaspoons baking powder
½	teaspoon salt
½	cup cold butter, cut into pieces
1½	cups shredded Cheddar cheese
1¼	cups whole milk

1. Preheat oven to 350°. Generously grease each cup of a 12-cup muffin pan with softened butter; set aside.

2. In a medium bowl, combine flour, cornmeal, sugar, baking powder, and salt. Using a pastry blender or fork, cut cold butter into flour mixture until crumbly. Stir in cheese. Add milk, stirring to mix well.

3. Place muffin pan in oven for 1 to 2 minutes, until butter is melted and pan is hot. Spoon batter into each muffin cup, filling about three-fourths full. Bake for 30 minutes or until rolls are golden brown.

Lemon Poppy Seed Mini Loaves
Makes 8 loaves

1	cup butter, softened
2	cups sugar
3	large eggs
4	cups all-purpose flour
2	teaspoons baking powder
½	teaspoon baking soda
¼	teaspoon salt
1	cup whole milk
½	cup sour cream
2	tablespoons poppy seeds
2	tablespoons lemon zest
1	teaspoon lemon extract
1	cup confectioners' sugar, sifted
2	tablespoons fresh lemon juice

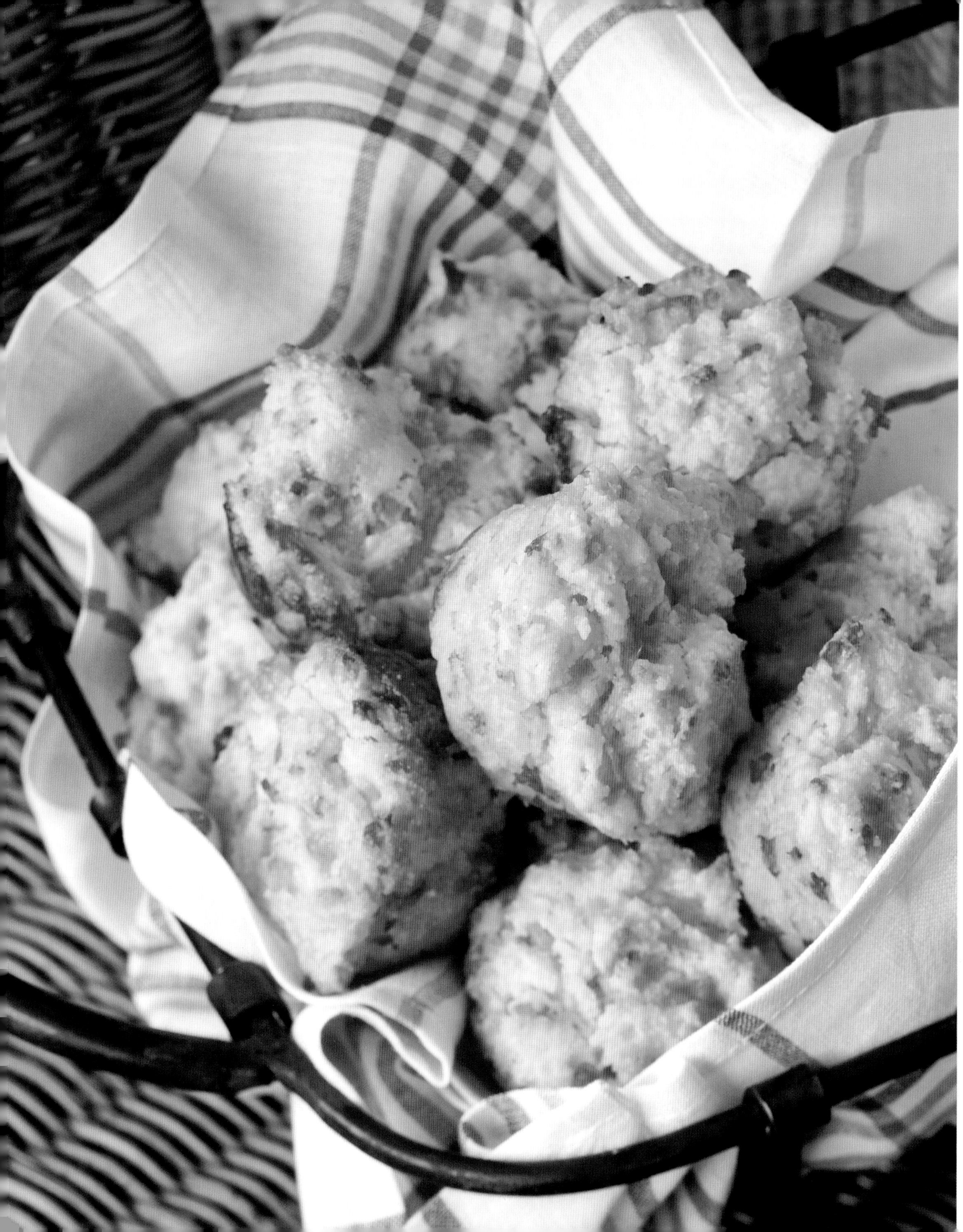

Fried Okra and Bacon Bites
Makes about 3 dozen

Vegetable oil for frying
1½ cups plain white cornmeal
1 cup self-rising flour
1 teaspoon salt
1 teaspoon garlic powder
½ teaspoon ground black pepper
½ pound fresh okra, finely chopped
6 slices bacon, cooked and crumbled
1 cup finely shredded Cheddar cheese
½ cup finely chopped green onion
1½ cups whole milk
1 large egg, lightly beaten
Dipping Sauce (recipe follows)

1. In a large Dutch oven, pour oil to a depth of 4 inches. Heat oil to 350°.

2. In a medium bowl, combine cornmeal, flour, salt, garlic powder, and pepper. Add okra, bacon, cheese, and green onion, stirring to combine.

3. In a small bowl, whisk together milk and egg. Combine milk mixture with cornmeal mixture. Drop batter by rounded tablespoons* into oil. Fry for 5 to 6 minutes or until golden brown. Drain on paper towels. Serve with Dipping Sauce.

To make bites perfectly round, use a 1 tablespoon cookie scoop.

DIPPING SAUCE
Makes about 1 cup

1 cup sour cream
2 tablespoons chopped fresh parsley
1 tablespoon Dijon mustard
2 teaspoons hot sauce
¼ teaspoon salt

1. In a small bowl, combine sour cream, parsley, Dijon, hot sauce, and salt, stirring to mix well. Store in an airtight container in refrigerator for up to 1 week.

Hoppin' John Cornbread

Makes 10 to 12 servings

- ¼ cup butter
- 4 cups self-rising buttermilk cornmeal mix
- 1 (15.5-ounce) can black-eyed peas, drained
- 1 (14.5-ounce) can fire-roasted tomatoes, drained
- 1 bunch green onions, chopped
- 10 slices bacon, cooked and crumbled
- 1 cup finely shredded sharp Cheddar cheese
- 2¾ cups whole buttermilk

1. Preheat oven to 425°. Place butter in a 10-inch cast-iron skillet; set aside.

2. In a large bowl, combine cornmeal mix, black-eyed peas, tomatoes, green onion, bacon, and cheese, stirring to combine. Stir in buttermilk.

3. Place skillet in oven for 4 to 5 minutes to melt butter and heat skillet. Spoon batter into hot skillet. Bake for 30 to 35 minutes or until golden brown. Let cool in pan for 5 minutes.

Lowcountry Love! Combine the flavors of two beloved dishes to create a delicious new Southern favorite.

Parmesan Garlic Crostini
Makes 2 dozen

1	(8-ounce) French baguette
¼	cup butter, melted
1¼	teaspoons garlic powder
½	cup finely grated Parmigiano-Reggiano cheese
2	tablespoons chopped fresh parsley

1. Preheat oven to 350°. Line a baking sheet with parchment paper.

2. Cut 24 (¼-inch-thick) slices from baguette.

3. In a small bowl, combine melted butter and garlic powder. Using a pastry brush, brush tops of bread slices with butter mixture. Sprinkle cheese evenly on tops of prepared slices. Sprinkle evenly with parsley. Place on prepared pan. Bake for 10 to 12 minutes.

Truffle Sage Buttered Baguettes
Makes 3 loaves

3	rustic French baguettes
	Truffle Sage Butter (recipe follows)
	Garnish: fresh sage

1. Preheat oven to 350°. Line baking sheets with parchment paper.

2. Using a bread knife, cut 1-inch slits in each baguette, being careful not to cut through bread. Spread about 1 to 2 teaspoons Truffle Sage Butter between each slit.

3. Bake until browned, 10 to 15 minutes. Remove from oven. Let cool slightly. Serve warm. Garnish with sage, if desired.

TRUFFLE SAGE BUTTER
Makes about 2 cups

1½	cups unsalted butter, softened
½	cup shredded Parmesan cheese
2	cloves garlic, minced
2	tablespoons fresh chopped sage
1	tablespoon fresh chopped oregano
1	tablespoon fresh chopped chives
1	tablespoon truffle oil
1	teaspoon kosher garlic salt
1	teaspoon ground black pepper

1. In the work bowl of a food processor, pulse together all ingredients until combined. Place in a resealable plastic container. Store covered in refrigerator for up to 1 week.

3

Savory
MAIN DISHES

*As the star of the dining experience, the main dish offers
delicious inspiration for the entire menu. These robust creations,
from classic casseroles to cheesy pastas—and even gourmet
grilled pizzas—are worthy of their turn in the spotlight.*

Grilled Chicken Pizza

Makes 1 large or 2 medium pizzas

Pizza Crust (recipe on page 155)
2   boneless skinless chicken breasts, cut into ½-inch-thick pieces
1   tablespoon olive oil
1   tablespoon Italian seasoning
1   teaspoon garlic powder
1   teaspoon salt
½   teaspoon ground black pepper
Roasted Pepper Sauce (recipe follows)
2½   cups shredded fontina cheese, divided
4   ounces sliced baby portobello mushrooms
1   cup baby spinach leaves
6   Campari tomatoes, sliced
¼   cup thinly sliced red onion

1. Spray grill rack with nonflammable cooking spray. Preheat grill to medium-high heat (350° to 400°).

2. Prepare Pizza Crust according to recipe directions, grilling one side of dough.

3. In a medium bowl, combine chicken, olive oil, Italian seasoning, garlic powder, salt, and pepper, tossing to coat. Using a grill pan, grill chicken over medium-high heat for 2 to 3 minutes per side; set aside.

4. Spread Roasted Pepper Sauce evenly over cooked side of crust.

Sprinkle evenly with 2 cups cheese. Layer chicken, mushrooms, spinach leaves, tomatoes, and red onion evenly over cheese. Sprinkle remaining ½ cup cheese over toppings.

5. Return pizza to grill, and grill over indirect heat for 7 to 10 minutes or until cheese is melted and bottom of crust is browned.

ROASTED PEPPER SAUCE
Makes about 1 cup

3   yellow bell peppers, halved and seeded
1   head garlic, roasted
½   teaspoon salt
¼   teaspoon ground black pepper

1. Preheat oven to 500°. Line a rimmed baking sheet with foil.

2. Place peppers skin side up on prepared pan. Bake for 30 minutes or until peppers appear blistered. Place peppers in a resealable plastic bag; seal, and let stand for 10 minutes to loosen skins. Remove skins from peppers, and discard skins.

3. In the work bowl of a food processor, combine peppers, roasted garlic, salt, and pepper. Process until smooth.

Note: To roast garlic, cut tops off heads of garlic, drizzle with olive oil, wrap in foil, and bake on 400° for 1 hour. Let garlic cool, and squeeze the garlic cloves out of their skins.

Grilled Mediterranean Pizza

Makes 1 large or 2 medium pizzas

　　Pizza Crust (recipe on page 155)
　　Fresh Pesto Sauce (recipe follows)
　8　ounces whole-milk mozzarella, thinly sliced
　½　cup diced roasted red peppers
　1　cup pitted green olives
　¾　cup pitted kalamata olives
　¼　cup crumbled feta cheese
　　Garnish: chopped fresh oregano

1. Spray grill rack with nonflammable cooking spray. Preheat grill to medium-high heat (350° to 400°). Prepare Pizza Crust according to recipe directions, grilling one side of dough. Spread Fresh Pesto Sauce evenly over cooked side of crust. Layer mozzarella, red peppers, and olives over pesto. Sprinkle feta cheese over toppings. Return pizza to grill, and grill over indirect heat for 7 to 10 minutes or until cheese is melted and bottom of crust is browned.

FRESH PESTO SAUCE

Makes about ½ cup

　1　(1-ounce) package fresh basil, stems removed
　½　cup freshly grated Parmigiano-Reggiano cheese
　¼　cup toasted pine nuts
　1½　teaspoons minced garlic
　3　tablespoons water
　2　tablespoons olive oil
　1　tablespoon fresh lemon juice
　¼　teaspoon ground black pepper

1. In the work bowl of a food processor, combine basil, cheese, pine nuts, and garlic. Process until well blended. Add water, olive oil, lemon juice, and pepper. Process until blended.

Homemade sauces and a made-from-scratch crust turn pizza night into something special.

Grilled Hawaiian Pizza with Spicy Barbecue Sauce
Makes 1 large pizza

Pizza Crust (see box)
Spicy Barbecue Sauce (recipe follows)
2½ cups finely shredded mozzarella cheese, divided
5 slices Canadian bacon, cut into pieces
2 cups diced fresh pineapple
4 slices hickory-smoked bacon, cooked and chopped
1 cup freshly grated Parmigiano-Reggiano cheese

1. Spray grill rack with nonflammable cooking spray. Preheat grill to medium-high heat (350° to 400°).

2. Prepare Pizza Crust according to recipe directions, grilling one side of dough. Spread Spicy Barbecue Sauce evenly over cooked side of crust. Sprinkle evenly with 2 cups mozzarella cheese. Layer Canadian bacon, pineapple, and bacon evenly over cheese. Sprinkle evenly with Parmigiano-Reggiano and remaining ½ cup mozzarella cheese.

3. Return pizza to grill, and grill over indirect heat for 7 to 10 minutes or until cheese is melted and bottom of crust is browned.

SPICY BARBECUE SAUCE
Makes about 1 cup

2 tablespoons butter
¼ cup finely chopped onion
½ cup water
½ cup ketchup
⅓ cup white vinegar
1½ tablespoons firmly packed dark brown sugar
1 tablespoon paprika
1 teaspoon Worcestershire sauce
1 teaspoon ground black pepper
½ teaspoon salt
¼ teaspoon ground red pepper (optional)

1. In a small saucepan, heat butter over medium heat until butter is melted. Add onion; cook for 2 minutes, stirring constantly. Add water, ketchup, vinegar, brown sugar, paprika, Worcestershire sauce, black pepper, salt, and red pepper (if desired), whisking to combine well. Reduce heat to medium-low; simmer for 30 to 40 minutes, stirring occasionally, until reduced to 1 cup.

Pizza Crust
Makes 1 large or 2 medium pizza crusts

¾ cup warm water (105° to 115°)
1 (0.25-ounce) package active dry yeast
1 teaspoon sugar
2½ cups all-purpose flour
1½ teaspoons salt
½ cup olive oil, divided
Yellow cornmeal

1. Combine water, yeast, and sugar in a 2-cup liquid measuring cup; let stand for 5 minutes.

2. In the work bowl of a food processor, combine flour and salt. Pulse several times to combine. With processor running, slowly add yeast mixture and ¼ cup olive oil. Continue running processor until mixture is combined and forms a ball.

3. On a lightly floured surface, turn out dough, and knead for 5 minutes. Place in a bowl coated with cooking spray, turning to coat top. Cover, and let rise in a warm (85°) place, free from drafts, for 1 hour or until dough is doubled in size.

4. Spray grill rack with nonflammable cooking spray. Preheat grill to medium-high heat (350° to 400°).

5. Sprinkle a clean flat surface heavily with cornmeal. For 1 large crust, roll dough into a ¼-inch-thick round or rectangle. For 2 medium crusts, divide dough in half, and roll each portion to ¼-inch-thick rounds or rectangles. Brush top(s) of crust(s) with 2 tablespoons olive oil. Sprinkle evenly with cornmeal. Place on grill, olive oil side down, and grill, covered with grill lid, for 3 to 4 minutes or until top of dough is bubbly and bottom of dough is browned. Brush top of crust(s) with remaining 2 tablespoons olive oil. Invert dough onto a pizza peel or a rimless baking sheet. Top cooked portion of dough with desired toppings. Return pizza to grill, and grill over indirect heat, covered with grill lid, for 7 to 10 minutes or until cheese is melted and bottom of crust is browned.

Chicken Piccata

Makes 4 servings

- 4   boneless skinless chicken breasts
- 1   cup plus 1 tablespoon all-purpose flour, divided
- 1¼   teaspoons salt, divided
- ¾   teaspoon ground black pepper, divided
- 8   tablespoons butter, divided
- 4   tablespoons olive oil, divided
- 3   tablespoons capers
- 1   tablespoon minced garlic
- ½   cup chicken broth
- ¼   cup dry white wine
- ¼   cup fresh lemon juice
- Garnish: lemon slices, fresh parsley

1. Preheat oven to 200°. Line a baking sheet with parchment paper.

2. Cut each chicken breast in half crosswise. Place each chicken breast between 2 sheets of plastic wrap; pound with a meat mallet to ⅛-inch thickness.

3. In a shallow dish, combine 1 cup flour, 1 teaspoon salt, and ½ teaspoon pepper. Dredge chicken in flour mixture, shaking off excess.

4. In a large nonstick skillet, heat 2 tablespoons butter and 2 tablespoons olive oil over medium-high heat. Add half of chicken; cook for 1½ to 2 minutes per side or until golden brown; repeat process with 2 tablespoons butter, remaining 2 tablespoons olive oil, and remaining half of chicken, wiping out skillet between batches. Place chicken on prepared pan, and place in oven to keep warm.

5. Return skillet to stovetop over medium heat. Add remaining 4 tablespoons butter; heat until melted. Add remaining 1 tablespoon flour; cook for 2 minutes, stirring constantly. Add capers and garlic, and cook for 1 minute. Add chicken broth, wine, lemon juice, remaining ¼ teaspoon salt, and remaining ¼ teaspoon pepper. Cook for 4 minutes, stirring frequently, until slightly thickened. Add chicken to pan, turning gently to coat chicken. Garnish with lemon slices and parsley, if desired.

Chicken and Wild Rice Casserole
Makes 10 to 12 servings

¼ cup butter
2 (8-ounce) containers sliced baby portobello mushrooms
4 cups chopped yellow onion
2 cups chopped celery
1 tablespoon minced garlic
6 cups cooked brown and wild rice*
4 cups chopped cooked chicken
1 (16-ounce) container sour cream
1 (10.75-ounce) can cream of chicken soup
2 tablespoons chopped fresh thyme
1 tablespoon chopped fresh rosemary
2 tablespoons dry sherry
2 teaspoons garlic powder
2 teaspoons salt
½ teaspoon ground black pepper

1. Preheat oven to 350°. Spray a 13x9-inch baking dish with cooking spray.

2. In a large Dutch oven, heat butter over medium heat until butter is melted. Add mushrooms, onion, celery, and garlic; cook for 20 minutes, stirring occasionally.

3. In a large bowl, combine rice, chicken, vegetable mixture, sour cream, soup, thyme, rosemary, sherry, garlic powder, salt, and pepper, stirring to combine well. Spoon rice mixture into prepared pan.

4. Bake for 40 to 45 minutes or until hot and bubbly. As an optional topping, combine 1 cup panko, 2 tablespoons olive oil, and 1 tablespoon parsley flakes. Sprinkle on top during last 10 minutes of cooking time.

We used Rice Select Royal Blend Whole Grain Texmati Brown and Wild Rice.

2. In a large bowl, combine chicken, spinach, cream cheese, green onion, and garlic powder. Beat with a mixer at medium speed until well combined. Spoon chicken mixture into manicotti, and place in prepared pan; set aside.

3. In a large saucepan, heat butter over medium heat until melted. Add flour, salt, and white pepper; cook for 2 minutes, whisking constantly. Gradually add milk, whisking constantly. Bring mixture to a simmer, and cook for 4 minutes, whisking constantly, until slightly thickened. Remove from heat, and add cheese, stirring until cheese melts. Spoon sauce over manicotti, and sprinkle evenly with Italian seasoning and pepper.

4. Bake for 35 to 40 minutes or until hot and bubbly.

Curry Chicken & Rice Casserole
Makes 10 to 12 servings

3	tablespoons olive oil
1	(8-ounce) container sliced baby portobello mushrooms
1	red bell pepper, chopped
1	large yellow onion, chopped
1	tablespoon minced garlic
8	cups chopped cooked chicken
6	cups cooked jasmine rice
1	(10-ounce) package frozen chopped broccoli, thawed
1	(16-ounce) container sour cream
1	(10.5-ounce) can cream of mushroom soup
3	cups shredded sharp Cheddar cheese, divided
1	cup shredded Swiss cheese
1	tablespoon fresh lemon juice
2	teaspoons curry powder
2	teaspoons salt
½	teaspoon ground black pepper

1. Preheat oven to 350°. Lightly grease a 3-quart baking dish with cooking spray.

2. In a large skillet, heat olive oil over medium heat. Add mushrooms, bell pepper, onion, and garlic; cook for 10 minutes, stirring frequently.

3. In a large bowl, combine chicken, mushroom mixture, rice, broccoli, sour cream, soup, 2 cups Cheddar cheese, Swiss cheese, lemon juice, curry powder, salt, and pepper, stirring to combine well. Spoon chicken mixture into prepared pan, and top with remaining 1 cup Cheddar cheese.

4. Bake for 45 minutes or until browned and bubbly. Serve immediately.

Chicken Florentine Manicotti Alfredo
Makes 6 to 8 servings

4	cups chopped cooked chicken
2½	cups chopped fresh spinach
2	(8-ounce) packages cream cheese, softened
¼	cup finely chopped green onion
1	teaspoon garlic powder
1	(8-ounce) package manicotti, cooked according to package directions
¼	cup butter
2	tablespoons all-purpose flour
½	teaspoon salt
¼	teaspoon ground white pepper
2	cups whole milk
1½	cups finely grated Parmigiano-Reggiano cheese
1	tablespoon Italian seasoning
½	teaspoon ground black pepper

1. Preheat oven to 350°. Spray a 13x9-inch baking dish with cooking spray.

occasionally, until pork is browned on all sides. Remove from heat. Pour chicken broth over pork.

5. In a large bowl, combine potatoes, carrots, and onions, remaining 2 tablespoons olive oil, remaining 2 teaspoons salt, and remaining ½ teaspoon pepper, tossing to coat. Place vegetables around pork in Dutch oven. Cover, and cook for 3 hours.

Mexican Lasagna
Makes 10 to 12 servings

2½ pounds ground chuck
1 large yellow onion, chopped
1   tablespoon minced garlic
1 (28-ounce) can crushed tomatoes
1 (28-ounce) can tomatoes with green chiles, drained
1 (6-ounce) can tomato paste
1 tablespoon ground cumin
2 teaspoons ground coriander
2 teaspoons chili powder
2 teaspoons salt, divided
1 teaspoon garlic powder
1 (16-ounce) container sour cream
1 (15-ounce) container ricotta cheese
2 large eggs
8 lasagna noodles, cooked
1 (16-ounce) block sharp Cheddar cheese, shredded
1 (8-ounce) block Monterey Jack cheese with peppers, shredded

1. In a large Dutch oven, combine ground beef, onion, and garlic over medium-high heat. Cook for 10 minutes or until browned. Add tomatoes, tomatoes with chiles, tomato paste, cumin, coriander, chili powder, 1½ teaspoons salt, and garlic powder. Reduce heat to low, and simmer, covered, for 45 minutes, stirring occasionally.

2. Preheat oven to 350°.

3. In a medium bowl, whisk together sour cream, ricotta cheese, eggs, and remaining ½ teaspoon salt.

4. Spread 2 cups meat sauce evenly over bottom of a 13x9x3-inch pan. Layer one-half lasagna noodles on top of meat sauce. Spread one-half remaining meat sauce on top of noodles. Top with one-half sour cream mixture and one-half cheeses. Repeat layers. Bake for 35 to 45 minutes or until browned and bubbly. Let stand for 15 minutes before serving.

Pork Roast with Vegetables
Makes 6 to 8 servings

1 (5-pound) fresh pork picnic shoulder, trimmed
6 tablespoons olive oil, divided
4 teaspoons coarse kosher salt, divided
2 teaspoons garlic powder
2 teaspoons onion powder
1 teaspoon ground black pepper, divided
1 cup all-purpose flour
2 cups chicken broth
2½ pounds red potatoes, cut into 2-inch pieces
2 pounds carrots, cut into 2-inch pieces
3 large yellow onions, cut into 2-inch pieces

1. Preheat oven to 325°. Rub pork shoulder with 1 tablespoon olive oil.

2. In a small bowl, combine 2 teaspoons salt, garlic powder, onion powder, and ½ teaspoon pepper. Rub entire pork shoulder with salt mixture.

3. Place flour in a shallow dish. Dredge pork on all sides with flour to coat completely.

4. In a large ovenproof Dutch oven, heat 3 tablespoons olive oil over medium-high heat; cook pork for 5 to 6 minutes, turning

Chicken Cordon Bleu Casserole

Makes 8 to 10 servings

---

  1 (10.75-ounce) can cream of chicken soup
1½ cups water
  1 (8-ounce) package Monterey Jack cheese, grated
  1 (8-ounce) package Swiss cheese, grated
  ¼ teaspoon ground black pepper
  2 (6.5-ounce) boxes garlic-and-butter-flavored rice*
1½ cups boiling water
  4 boneless skinless chicken breasts, cut into
       ½-inch slices
  1 (3.5-ounce) package prosciutto, chopped
Garnish: chopped fresh parsley

1. Preheat oven to 375°.

2. In a large saucepan, combine soup and water over medium-high heat; bring to a simmer. Reduce heat to low. Add cheeses, stirring until melted. Stir in pepper. Remove from heat, and set aside.

3. Pour rice into an ungreased 13x9-inch baking dish. Pour boiling water over rice; spread rice evenly over bottom of dish. Spoon half of soup mixture over rice. Layer chicken and prosciutto evenly over top of soup mixture; top with remaining soup mixture. Bake, uncovered, for 1 hour. Let stand for 10 minutes before serving. Garnish with parsley, if desired.

We used Zatarain's Garlic Butter Flavored Rice.

Baked Spaghetti
Makes 8 to 10 servings

- 2 **pounds ground chuck**
- 1 **yellow onion, chopped**
- 1 **(8-ounce) package sliced baby portobello mushrooms**
- 1 **tablespoon minced garlic**
- 1 **(28-ounce) can crushed tomatoes**
- 1 **(14.5-ounce) can fire-roasted diced tomatoes, undrained**
- 1 **(6-ounce) can tomato paste**
- 2 **tablespoons Italian seasoning**
- 1 **tablespoon garlic powder**
- 1 **tablespoon sugar**
- 2½ **teaspoons salt, divided**
- 1 **(15-ounce) container ricotta cheese**
- 2½ **cups finely grated Parmesan cheese, divided**
- 1 **(16-ounce) package thin spaghetti, cooked**
- 3 **cups shredded mozzarella cheese, divided**

1. Preheat oven to 350°.

2. In a large Dutch oven, combine ground chuck, onion, mushrooms, and garlic over medium-high heat; cook for 10 to 15 minutes, stirring occasionally, until browned. Remove meat mixture from pan; drain and return to pan. Add tomatoes, tomato paste, Italian seasoning, garlic powder, sugar, and 2 teaspoons salt.

3. In a medium bowl, combine ricotta, 2 cups Parmesan cheese, and remaining ½ teaspoon salt, stirring to combine well.

4. Spread 2 cups meat sauce in the bottom of a 3½-quart baking dish. Layer half of spaghetti noodles on top of meat sauce. Spread half of remaining meat sauce on top of noodles. Spread ricotta mixture on top of meat sauce. Sprinkle 2 cups mozzarella cheese on top of ricotta mixture. Layer remaining half of noodles and remaining meat sauce on top of mozzarella. Sprinkle remaining 1 cup mozzarella and ½ cup Parmesan on top of meat sauce.

5. Bake for 35 to 40 minutes, and serve immediately.

> *"One cannot think well, love well, sleep well, if one has not dined well."*
> —Virginia Woolf

Chicken Enchiladas
Makes 8 servings

8   cups chopped cooked chicken
1   (28-ounce) can tomatoes with green chiles, well drained
1   (15-ounce) can black beans, rinsed and drained
1   (10.75-ounce) can cream of chicken soup
3   cups shredded Monterey Jack cheese, divided
1   cup sour cream
2   teaspoons ground cumin
2   teaspoons garlic powder
1   teaspoon chili powder
1   teaspoon salt
8   medium soft taco flour tortillas
1   (10-ounce) can mild green chile enchilada sauce

1. Preheat oven to 350°. Spray a 13x9-inch baking dish with cooking spray.

2. In a large bowl, combine chicken, tomatoes with chiles, black beans, soup, 2 cups cheese, sour cream, cumin, garlic powder, chili powder, and salt, stirring to combine well. Spoon 1 cup chicken mixture down center of each tortilla; roll up tortilla tightly. Place enchiladas, seam side down, in a single layer in prepared pan; top with enchilada sauce. Sprinkle evenly with remaining 1 cup cheese.

3. Bake for 30 to 35 minutes or until hot and bubbly. Serve immediately.

4

Delicious
SALADS AND SOUPS

In this busy day and age when time is a precious commodity, it's especially advantageous to have a go-to cache of tried-and-true dishes that are easy and nutritious. From dressing-drizzled greens and crisp veggie side salads to soul-warming soups and stews, these recipes can be delicious accompaniments to the menu or compose a meal on their own.

1. In a small bowl, combine vinegar, sugar, salt, garlic powder, and pepper, whisking until sugar dissolves. Gradually add olive oil, whisking to combine well. Store in an airtight container in refrigerator for up to 1 week.

Watercress Salad with Ginger Pomegranate Dressing

Makes 6 to 8 servings

2 (4-ounce) bags watercress, tough stems removed
1 (4-ounce) bag arugula
1 (6-ounce) bag radishes, thinly sliced
4 large oranges, sectioned
2 shallots, thinly sliced
Ginger Pomegranate Dressing (recipe follows)
1 (4-ounce) container goat cheese crumbles
Garnish: chopped toasted walnuts

1. In a large bowl, combine watercress, arugula, radishes, orange sections, and shallot, tossing gently to combine. Drizzle with Ginger Pomegranate Dressing just before serving. Top with goat cheese crumbles; garnish with walnuts, if desired.

GINGER POMEGRANATE DRESSING
Makes 1¾ cups

¾ cup pomegranate juice*
¼ cup white wine vinegar
1 teaspoon minced ginger
1 tablespoon sugar
¾ teaspoon salt
½ teaspoon ground black pepper
½ cup extra-light olive oil

1. In a small bowl, combine pomegranate juice, vinegar, ginger, sugar, salt, and pepper, whisking until sugar dissolves. Gradually add olive oil, whisking to combine. Cover, and refrigerate until ready to serve.

2. To serve, bring to room temperature. Store in an airtight container for up to 2 weeks.

We used POM Wonderful 100% Pomegranate Juice.

Fall Salad with Red Wine Vinaigrette

Makes 4 servings

1 head red leaf lettuce, washed, dried, and torn
1 head endive
2 cups shaved fennel
1 Granny Smith apple, thinly sliced
Red Wine Vinaigrette (recipe follows)
Garnish: toasted pine nuts

1. Divide lettuce, endive, fennel, and apple among four salad plates. Drizzle with Red Wine Vinaigrette. Garnish with toasted pine nuts, if desired.

RED WINE VINAIGRETTE
Makes about 2 cups

1 cup red wine vinegar
2 teaspoons sugar
½ teaspoon salt
½ teaspoon garlic powder
½ teaspoon ground black pepper
¾ cup extra-light olive oil

Winter Salad with Creamy Thyme Dressing

Makes 8 servings

- 1 head red leaf lettuce, washed, dried, and torn
- 1 head endive, leaves separated
- ½ head radicchio, thinly sliced
- 1 cup dried cranberries
- 1 red pear, thinly sliced
- 1 green pear, thinly sliced

Creamy Thyme Dressing (recipe follows)

Garnish: toasted walnuts

1. In a large bowl, combine lettuce, endive, radicchio, and cranberries. Divide among 8 salad plates. Top with pear slices. Drizzle with Creamy Thyme Dressing. Garnish with walnuts, if desired.

CREAMY THYME DRESSING

Makes about 2½ cups

- 2 cups mayonnaise
- ½ cup whole buttermilk
- ¼ cup white wine vinegar
- 3 tablespoons chopped fresh thyme
- 1 tablespoon Dijon mustard
- ½ teaspoon garlic powder
- ½ teaspoon ground black pepper
- ¼ teaspoon garlic salt

1. In a medium bowl, combine mayonnaise, buttermilk, vinegar, thyme, Dijon, garlic powder, pepper, and salt, whisking to combine well. Store in an airtight container in the refrigerator for up to 1 week.

Hearts of Palm Salad

Makes 8 to 10 servings

- ¼ cup fresh lemon juice
- 2 tablespoons fresh lime juice
- 1 tablespoon honey
- 1 teaspoon garlic powder
- ¾ teaspoon salt
- ½ teaspoon ground black pepper
- ¼ cup extra-light olive oil
- 4 (14-ounce) cans hearts of palm, drained and sliced
- 4 avocados, peeled and diced
- 1 (1-pound) container Campari tomatoes, quartered
- 1 English cucumber, diced
- 1 shallot, minced
- ¼ cup chopped fresh cilantro

1. In a small bowl, combine lemon juice, lime juice, honey, garlic powder, salt, and pepper, whisking until honey dissolves. Whisking constantly, slowly drizzle in olive oil.

2. In a large bowl, combine hearts of palm, avocados, tomatoes, cucumber, shallot, and cilantro. Add lemon juice mixture to hearts of palm mixture, tossing gently to coat.

Smokey Roasted
Red Pepper Soup

Makes 10 to 12 servings

8	large red bell peppers, halved and seeded
2	tablespoons olive oil
3	cups chopped yellow onion
1	tablespoon minced garlic
2	tablespoons tomato paste
2	quarts chicken broth
1½	cups heavy whipping cream
1	teaspoon salt
1	teaspoon sugar
½	teaspoon smoked paprika
½	teaspoon garlic powder
½	teaspoon ground black pepper
1	(8-ounce) package smoked Gouda cheese, shredded

1. Preheat oven to 500°.

2. Line a rimmed baking sheet with foil, and spray foil with cooking spray. Place peppers skin side up on prepared pan. Bake for 30 minutes or until peppers appear blistered. Place peppers in a resealable plastic bag; seal, and let stand for 10 minutes to loosen skins. Remove skins from peppers, and chop.

3. In a large Dutch oven, heat olive oil over medium heat. Add onion and garlic; cook for 6 minutes, stirring occasionally, until tender. Add tomato paste; cook for 2 minutes, stirring constantly. Add chicken broth and reserved bell pepper; bring to a simmer. Remove from heat, and let cool slightly.

4. In the container of a blender, purée red pepper mixture in batches until smooth. Return red pepper mixture to Dutch oven over medium-low heat. Add cream, salt, sugar, smoked paprika, garlic powder, and pepper, whisking until smooth; cook for 10 minutes. Stir in cheese until melted.

Smoked Sausage and White Bean Soup

Makes 10 to 12 servings

2   tablespoons olive oil
1   tablespoon minced garlic
2   pounds hickory-smoked sausage, cut into 1-inch pieces
1   large yellow onion, chopped
2   quarts chicken broth
4   (15.5-ounce) cans cannellini beans, undrained
3   (15.5-ounce) cans navy beans, undrained
2   cups chopped carrot
1   cup chopped celery
1   teaspoon garlic powder
½   teaspoon salt
¼   teaspoon ground black pepper
1   (6-ounce) bag baby spinach

1. In a large Dutch oven, heat olive oil over medium heat. Add garlic; cook for 1 minute, stirring constantly. Add sausage and onion; cook for 20 minutes, stirring frequently, until sausage is lightly browned. Add chicken broth, beans, carrot, celery, garlic powder, salt, and pepper. Bring to a boil over medium-high heat. Reduce heat, and simmer, uncovered, for 1 hour, stirring occasionally. Add spinach; cook for 2 to 3 minutes, stirring constantly, until spinach is wilted.

Beef Stroganoff Soup

Makes 10 to 12 servings

- ¼ cup olive oil
- 2 large yellow onions, sliced into ½-inch strips
- 2 (8-ounce) containers sliced baby portobello mushrooms
- 1 tablespoon minced garlic
- 3 pounds top round steak, sliced into 1x½-inch pieces
- 3 quarts beef broth
- 2 (10.5-ounce) cans beef consommé
- 2 teaspoons Worcestershire sauce
- 1 teaspoon salt
- ½ teaspoon ground black pepper
- ½ (16-ounce) package wide egg noodles
- 1 (8-ounce) package Fontina cheese, shredded
- 1 cup sour cream
- 1 tablespoon chopped fresh thyme
- Garnish: chopped fresh thyme

1. In a large Dutch oven, heat olive oil over medium heat. Add onion, mushrooms, and garlic; cook for 20 minutes, stirring frequently. Add steak; cook for 10 minutes, stirring frequently, until browned. Add beef broth, consommé, Worcestershire sauce, salt, and pepper. Bring to a boil over medium-high heat; reduce heat, and simmer, covered, for 2 hours or until meat is tender, stirring occasionally. Add egg noodles; cook for 10 to 12 minutes or until noodles are tender. Remove from heat; add cheese, sour cream, and thyme. Whisk until smooth and cheese is melted. Garnish with thyme, if desired.

Spaghetti and Meatball Soup

Makes 10 to 12 servings

- 2 pounds ground chuck
- 5 tablespoons Italian seasoning, divided
- 2 tablespoons minced garlic, divided
- 2¼ teaspoons salt, divided
- 1 teaspoon ground black pepper, divided
- 2 cups panko (Japanese bread crumbs)
- 1 cup finely grated Parmesan cheese
- 3 large eggs, lightly beaten
- 2 tablespoons olive oil
- 1 large yellow onion, chopped
- 1 large green bell pepper, chopped
- 1 cup chopped celery
- 2 quarts beef broth
- 2 (28-ounce) cans crushed tomatoes
- 2 (14.5-ounce) cans fire-roasted diced tomatoes
- 2 tablespoons sugar

- 2 teaspoons garlic powder
- 8 ounces uncooked spaghetti noodles, broken into pieces
- Garnish: finely grated Parmesan cheese, chopped fresh basil

1. In a large bowl, combine ground chuck, 2 tablespoons Italian seasoning, 1 tablespoon minced garlic, ¾ teaspoon salt, and ½ teaspoon pepper, stirring well to combine. Add panko, Parmesan cheese, and eggs, mixing well to combine.

2. Line a rimmed baking sheet with foil.

3. Roll meat mixture into 1½-inch balls, and place on prepared pan. Cover, and refrigerate for 30 minutes.

4. In a large Dutch oven, heat olive oil over medium heat. Add onion, bell pepper, celery, and remaining 1 tablespoon minced garlic; cook for 10 minutes, stirring frequently. Add beef broth, tomatoes, remaining 3 tablespoons Italian seasoning, sugar, garlic powder, remaining 1½ teaspoons salt, and remaining ½ teaspoon pepper. Bring to a boil over medium-high heat. Carefully add meatballs to Dutch oven; do not stir. Reduce heat to medium, and simmer, covered, for 30 minutes. Skim and discard any fat. Add spaghetti noodles, and cook for 10 to 12 minutes or until pasta is tender. Garnish with Parmesan cheese and basil, if desired.

Peanut Soup with Sippets

Makes 10 to 12 servings

- ¼ cup butter
- 2½ cups finely chopped yellow onion
- 1½ cups finely chopped celery
- 1 tablespoon minced garlic
- 3 tablespoons all-purpose flour
- 2 quarts chicken broth
- 2½ cups creamy peanut butter
- ½ cup heavy whipping cream
- ¼ teaspoon garlic powder
- ¼ teaspoon ground red pepper
- Sippets (recipe follows)
- Garnish: chopped roasted salted peanuts, cooked crumbled bacon

1. In a large Dutch oven, heat butter over medium heat until melted. Add onion, celery, and garlic; cook for 10 minutes, stirring frequently, until tender. Add flour; cook for 2 minutes, stirring constantly. Gradually add chicken broth, stirring until well combined. Bring to a boil over medium-high heat; reduce heat, and simmer for 20 minutes. Remove from heat, and let cool for 10 minutes.

2. In the container of a blender, purée mixture in batches until smooth. Return mixture to Dutch oven over medium heat. Add peanut butter, cream, garlic powder, and red pepper, whisking until smooth. Cook for 5 minutes or until just heated through. Serve with Sippets. Garnish with peanuts and bacon, if desired.

SIPPETS
Makes 2 dozen

- 1 (8.5-ounce) French baguette
- 6 tablespoons butter, melted
- ½ teaspoon garlic powder
- ½ teaspoon seasoned salt

1. Preheat oven to 350°. Line a baking sheet with parchment paper.

2. Cut 24 (½-inch-thick) slices from baguette. Brush both sides with melted butter. Sprinkle tops evenly with garlic powder and seasoned salt. Bake for 12 minutes or until lightly browned.

Vegetable Soup

Makes about 6½ quarts

- 3 quarts chicken broth
- 2 pounds red potatoes, cut into 1-inch pieces
- 1 pound carrots, cut into 1-inch pieces
- 1 large yellow onion, cut into 1-inch pieces
- 1 stalk celery, peeled and chopped
- 1 (2-pound) bag frozen baby lima beans
- 1 (1-pound) bag frozen niblet corn
- 1 (28-ounce) can crushed tomatoes
- 2 (14.5-ounce) cans fire-roasted diced tomatoes
- 3 tablespoons garlic powder
- 1½ tablespoons salt
- 1 tablespoon sugar
- 1 tablespoon Worcestershire sauce
- 1½ to 2 teaspoons ground black pepper

1. In a large stockpot, combine chicken broth, potatoes, carrots, onion, celery, lima beans, corn, tomatoes, garlic powder, salt, sugar, Worcestershire sauce, and pepper. Bring to a boil over medium-high heat. Reduce heat to medium-low; simmer, uncovered, for 2 hours, stirring occasionally. (Note: This soup freezes well.)

Beefy Minestrone

Makes about 5 quarts

6	tablespoons olive oil, divided
3	pounds (1-inch) beef tips
3	cups chopped yellow onion
1½	cups chopped carrot
1½	cups chopped celery
1	leek, thinly sliced
1	tablespoon minced garlic
3	quarts beef broth
2	(10.5-ounce) cans beef consommé
1	(28-ounce) can diced tomatoes, undrained
1	Parmesan cheese rind (about 4x2 inches)
2	tablespoons Italian seasoning
1½	teaspoons salt
1	teaspoon ground black pepper
½	teaspoon crushed red pepper
2	cups diced zucchini
2	(15.5-ounce) cans cannellini beans, drained
1	cup ditalini pasta
Grated Parmesan cheese	

1. In a large Dutch oven, heat 4 tablespoons olive oil over medium heat. Add beef tips, in batches if necessary. Cook for 10 to 12 minutes, stirring frequently, until browned. Remove meat from Dutch oven, drain, and set aside.

2. In Dutch oven, heat remaining 2 tablespoons olive oil over medium heat. Add onion, carrot, celery, leek, and garlic; cook for 6 to 8 minutes, stirring frequently. Add beef broth, consommé, tomatoes, cheese rind, Italian seasoning, salt, black pepper, red pepper, and reserved meat. Bring to a boil; reduce heat to medium-low, and simmer, uncovered, for 1 hour, stirring occasionally.

3. Increase heat to medium. Add zucchini and beans; cook for 15 minutes, stirring occasionally. Add pasta; cook for 10 to 12 minutes or until pasta is tender. Remove and discard cheese rind. Serve with Parmesan cheese.

Southwest Chicken Soup

Makes 10 to 12 servings

4   quarts chicken broth
3   (10-ounce) cans diced tomatoes with green chiles
2   zucchini squash, halved lengthwise and thinly sliced
1   large yellow onion, chopped
1   cup chopped celery
1   cup chopped carrots
2   jalapeños, seeded and minced
½   medium cabbage, chopped
4   cups chopped cooked chicken
½   cup chopped fresh cilantro
¼   cup fresh lime juice

1   tablespoon ground cumin
1   tablespoon hot sauce
1   teaspoon garlic powder
1   teaspoon chili powder
1   teaspoon salt
Garnish: sour cream, chopped fresh cilantro

1. In a large Dutch oven, combine chicken broth, tomatoes, zucchini, onion, celery, carrot, jalapeño, and cabbage. Bring to a boil over medium-high heat; reduce heat, and simmer for 30 minutes or until vegetables are tender. Add chicken, cilantro, lime juice, cumin, hot sauce, garlic powder, chili powder, and salt; cook for 10 minutes or until heated through. Garnish with sour cream and cilantro, if desired. Serve with tortilla chips.

5

Delectable
SIDE DISHES

Much more than just the supporting cast for the entrée, side dishes shine in a light all their own. A colorful tumble of bacon-topped succotash, a Mediterranean spin on spaghetti squash—these savory sides offer their own tempting contributions to the success of the meal.

"The greatest delight the fields and woods minister is the suggestion of an occult relation between man and the vegetable. I am not alone and unacknowledged. They nod to me and I to them."
—Ralph Waldo Emerson

Ratatouille

Makes 10 to 12 servings

¼	cup olive oil
1	large red onion, chopped
1	tablespoon minced garlic
2	zucchini squash, diced
2	yellow squash, diced
1	large eggplant, diced
1	large red bell pepper, chopped
1½	teaspoons salt
¼	teaspoon ground black pepper
2	(14.5-ounce) cans fire-roasted diced tomatoes, (1 drained, 1 undrained)
2	tablespoons balsamic glace*
1	tablespoon chopped fresh parsley
1	tablespoon chopped fresh thyme
1	tablespoon chopped fresh basil

Garnish: freshly grated Parmesan cheese

1. In a large skillet, heat olive oil over medium heat. Add onion and garlic; cook for 10 minutes. Add squashes, eggplant, bell pepper, salt, and pepper; cook for 10 minutes, stirring frequently. Add tomatoes, balsamic glace, parsley, thyme, and basil; cook for 10 minutes, stirring occasionally. Garnish with Parmesan cheese, if desired.

We used Colavita Balsamic Glace.

Orange-Glazed Carrots with Tarragon

Makes 6 to 8 servings

- 2 tablespoons butter
- 2 shallots, thinly sliced
- 1 tablespoon minced garlic
- 1 cup fresh orange juice
- 1 tablespoon honey
- ¾ teaspoon salt
- ½ teaspoon ground black pepper
- 2 pounds carrots, sliced ¼ inch thick
- 2 tablespoons olive oil
- 2 tablespoons chopped fresh tarragon

1. Preheat oven to 450°. Line a rimmed baking sheet with foil.

2. In a small saucepan, heat butter over medium heat until melted. Add shallot and garlic; cook for 2 minutes, stirring frequently. Add orange juice, honey, salt, and pepper, stirring to combine. Cook over medium-high heat for 10 to 12 minutes, stirring occasionally, until mixture is slightly thickened.

3. In a medium bowl, combine carrots and olive oil, tossing gently to coat. Arrange carrots in a single layer on prepared pan. Bake for 10 minutes. Pour glaze over carrots, stirring gently to coat. Bake for 5 minutes or until carrots are crisp tender and glaze is thickened. Let stand in pan for 2 minutes. Add tarragon, tossing to combine.

Sweet Potatoes Au Gratin
Makes 8 to 10 servings

- 1 cup heavy whipping cream
- 1½ teaspoons salt
- ½ teaspoon ground black pepper
- 1½ cups grated Parmesan cheese
- 1½ cups shredded Monterey Jack cheese
- 3 pounds sweet potatoes, peeled and thinly sliced

Garnish: chopped fresh rosemary

1. Preheat to 400°.

2. In a small bowl, combine cream, salt, and pepper; whisk until salt dissolves.

3. In a separate bowl, combine cheeses.

4. In a 9x9-inch baking dish, layer half of sweet potatoes, half of cheese, and half of cream mixture; repeat layers. Cover with aluminum foil, and bake for 1½ hours. Remove foil, and continue baking for 15 to 20 minutes or until sweet potatoes are tender. Let stand for 15 minutes before serving. Garnish with rosemary, if desired.

Balsamic Green Beans and Caramelized Shallots
Makes 6 servings

- 5 tablespoons olive oil, divided
- 8 shallots, quartered lengthwise
- ½ cup balsamic vinegar, divided
- 1 teaspoon salt, divided
- ½ teaspoon ground black pepper, divided
- 3 (8-ounce) bags French green beans
- ¼ cup butter
- 1 tablespoon firmly packed dark brown sugar
- 1 tablespoon minced garlic

Garnish: toasted sliced almonds

1. In a large nonstick skillet, heat 2 tablespoons olive oil over medium-high heat. Add shallots, ¼ cup balsamic vinegar, ½ teaspoon salt, and ¼ teaspoon pepper. Cook for 5 to 6 minutes, stirring occasionally. Remove from skillet, and set aside.

2. In skillet, heat remaining 3 tablespoons olive oil over medium-high heat. Add green beans; cook for 10 minutes, stirring frequently. Add remaining ¼ cup balsamic vinegar, remaining ½ teaspoon salt, remaining ¼ teaspoon pepper, butter, brown sugar, and garlic, stirring until butter is melted. Add reserved shallot; cook for 1 minute until heated through. Garnish with almonds, if desired.

Old-Fashioned Turnip Greens
Makes 10 to 12 servings

- 2 tablespoons olive oil
- 6 slices thick-cut bacon, cut into 1-inch pieces
- 1 large onion, chopped
- 3 garlic cloves, cut in half
- 2 (1-pound) bags cut and washed turnip greens
- 2 quarts chicken broth
- 2 quarts water
- 1 ham hock
- 2 dried chile peppers
- 2 bay leaves
- 1 tablespoon kosher salt
- 1 tablespoon sugar
- ⅓ cup apple-cider vinegar

1. In a large Dutch oven, heat olive oil over medium heat. Add bacon; cook until browned, about 8 to 10 minutes. Add onion and garlic; cook for 10 minutes, stirring occasionally, until lightly browned. Add turnip greens, 1 bag at a time, and wilt, stirring often. Add broth, water, ham hock, peppers, bay leaves, salt, sugar, and vinegar. Bring to a boil over medium-high heat. Reduce heat, and cook, covered, for 20 minutes, stirring occasionally. Uncover, and cook for 15 to 20 minutes. Remove peppers and bay leaves, and discard.

Mediterranean Spaghetti Squash
Makes 6 to 8 servings

- 2 spaghetti squash, halved lengthwise and seeded
- 2 tablespoons olive oil
- 1 (7-ounce) jar pitted kalamata olives, drained
- 1 bunch green onions, chopped
- 2 tablespoons fresh lemon juice
- 1 tablespoon minced garlic
- 1 teaspoon salt
- ½ teaspoon garlic powder
- ¼ teaspoon crushed red pepper
- ¼ teaspoon ground black pepper
- 1 pint grape tomatoes, halved
- Garnish: crumbled feta cheese, chopped fresh oregano

1. Preheat oven to 350°. Line a baking sheet with foil, and spray with cooking spray.

2. Place squash cut side down on prepared pan. Bake for 30 minutes. Remove squash from oven, and let cool for 10 minutes.

3. In a large skillet, heat olive oil over medium heat. Add olives, green onion, lemon juice, garlic, salt, garlic powder, red pepper, and black pepper. Cook for 3 minutes, stirring occasionally. Add tomatoes; cook for 1 minute or just until tomatoes are heated through. Remove from heat.

4. Using a spoon, scoop stringy pulp from squash into a medium bowl. Top with olive mixture. Garnish with feta cheese and oregano, if desired.

SIDE DISHES

187

2. In a large saucepan, combine milk, half-and-half, salt, and sugar. Bring to a simmer over medium heat. Gradually add flour, whisking constantly, until well combined. Cook for 1 minute, whisking constantly. Remove from heat, and add butter, whisking until butter melts.

3. In a medium bowl, beat egg yolks with a mixer at medium speed for 2 minutes or until pale yellow in color. Add flour mixture, sweet potato, cheese, and rosemary, whisking well to combine.

4. In a medium bowl, beat egg whites with a mixer at high speed until stiff peaks form. Gently fold together egg whites and sweet potato mixture. Evenly divide sweet potato mixture among prepared ramekins. Bake for 30 to 35 minutes or until lightly browned.

Summer Succotash
Makes 10 to 12 servings

3	cups fresh or frozen baby lima beans
2	tablespoons olive oil
2	tablespoons butter
1	bunch green onions, chopped
1	tablespoon minced garlic
4	cups fresh yellow corn kernels (about 6 ears)
2	zucchini squash, diced
2	cups heavy whipping cream
1½	tablespoons chopped fresh thyme
1½	teaspoons salt
½	teaspoon ground black pepper
1	pint grape tomatoes, halved
1	pound thick-sliced peppered bacon, cooked and crumbled

1. In a medium saucepan, combine lima beans with enough water to cover. Bring to a boil over medium-high heat, reduce heat, and simmer for 10 to 15 minutes or until beans are tender. Drain, and set aside.

2. In a Dutch oven, heat olive oil and butter over medium heat until butter melts. Add green onion and garlic; cook for 3 to 4 minutes, stirring frequently. Add corn, zucchini, lima beans, cream, thyme, salt, and pepper; cook for 20 minutes, stirring occasionally. Add tomatoes; cook for 1 to 2 minutes, just until tomatoes are heated through. Top with crumbled bacon.

Savory Sweet Potato Soufflés
Makes 8 servings

½	cup panko (Japanese bread crumbs)
1½	cups whole milk
1	cup half-and-half
1¼	teaspoons salt
1	teaspoon sugar
½	cup all-purpose flour
¼	cup butter, cut into pieces
4	large eggs, separated
1½	cups cooked mashed sweet potato
1½	cups grated Gruyère cheese
1	tablespoon chopped fresh rosemary

1. Preheat oven to 375°. Spray 8 (1-cup) ramekins with cooking spray. Sprinkle evenly with panko, tilting and turning dishes to coat sides completely. Place prepared ramekins on a rimmed baking sheet.

6

Heavenly DESSERTS

Southerners love to finish off a meal with a sugary flourish. From tender cakes and flaky pies to warm, comforting fruit crisps—and every mouthwatering confection in between—desserts offer a sweet finale to any occasion.

4. On a floured surface, roll half of Lemon Crust into a 12-inch circle. Place in a 9-inch deep-dish pie plate. Trim excess pastry ½ inch beyond edge of pie plate. Place cherry mixture in prepared crust.

5. Roll remaining Lemon Crust to ⅛-inch thickness. Using a pastry wheel or knife, cut into ½-inch-wide strips. Arrange in a lattice design over cherry mixture. Trim strips even with edges. Press edges of crust together. Fold edges under, and crimp.

6. Brush crust with milk, and sprinkle with remaining 1 teaspoon granulated sugar. Bake for 45 minutes. Loosely cover with foil, and bake 45 minutes more or until lightly browned and bubbly.

LEMON CRUST
Makes 1 double pie crust

- 3   cups all-purpose flour
- 2   teaspoons lemon zest
- 1   teaspoon salt
- ⅓   cup shortening
- ⅓   cup cold butter, cut into pieces
- 8   to 10 tablespoons cold water

1. In the work bowl of a food processor, combine flour, lemon zest, and salt; pulse until well combined. Add shortening and butter; pulse until mixture is crumbly.

2. With processor running, add cold water, 1 tablespoon at a time, until mixture forms a ball. Divide dough in half, and flatten into two disks. Wrap tightly in plastic wrap; refrigerate for 1 hour.

Deep-Dish Cherry Pie
Makes 1 (9-inch) deep-dish pie

- 6   tablespoons instant tapioca
- ½   cup plus 1 teaspoon granulated sugar, divided
- ½   cup firmly packed light brown sugar
- ⅛   teaspoon salt
- 8   cups pitted Bing cherries
- 2   tablespoons fresh lemon juice
- Lemon Crust (recipe follows)
- 1   tablespoon milk

1. Preheat oven to 350°.

2. Using a spice grinder, finely grind tapioca.

3. In a large bowl, combine ½ cup granulated sugar, brown sugar, tapioca, and salt. Add cherries and lemon juice, tossing to coat.

Apple Butter Pound Cake
Makes 12 servings

- 1   cup apple butter
- 1¼   cup firmly packed light brown sugar, divided
- ½   cup chopped pecans
- 1½   cups unsalted butter, softened
- 1   (8-ounce) package cream cheese, softened
- 2   cups granulated sugar
- 1½   teaspoons kosher salt
- 5   large eggs, room temperature
- 1   tablespoon vanilla extract

  3   cups all-purpose flour
  1   teaspoon ground cinnamon
  ½   teaspoon baking powder
      Glaze (recipe follows)

1. Spray a 15-cup Bundt pan with baking spray with flour.

2. In a medium bowl, stir together apple butter, ¼ cup brown sugar, and pecans. Set aside.

3. In a large bowl, beat butter and cream cheese with a mixer at medium-high speed for 3 to 4 minutes or until smooth. Add remaining 1 cup brown sugar, granulated sugar, and salt; beat at high speed for 10 minutes, stopping occasionally to scrape down sides of bowl. Add eggs, one at a time, beating well after each addition. Beat in vanilla. Gradually add flour, cinnamon, and baking powder, beating until well combined.

4. Spoon one-third of batter into prepared pan. Spoon half of apple butter mixture over batter in pan. Top with another third of batter, remaining half of apple butter, and remaining batter. Using a knife, pull blade back and forth through batter to swirl apple butter layers. Smooth top with an offset spatula.

5. Place in a cold oven. Bake at 300° until a wooden pick inserted in center comes out clean, about 1 hour and 20 minutes. Let cool in pan for 10 minutes. Remove from pan, and let cool completely on a wire rack. Drizzle with Glaze.

GLAZE
Makes about 2 cups

  ½   cup unsalted butter
  1   cup firmly packed light brown sugar
  ²⁄₃ cup heavy whipping cream
  1   teaspoon vanilla extract
  ¼   teaspoon kosher salt
  1½ cups confectioners' sugar, sifted

1. In a medium saucepan, combine butter, brown sugar, cream, vanilla, and salt. Bring to a boil over medium-high heat, stirring constantly, until sugar is dissolved, about 3 minutes. Remove from heat, and let cool for 10 minutes. Whisk in confectioners' sugar.

Pecan Frangipane (recipe follows)
1 large egg, lightly beaten
1 tablespoon water
2 tablespoons coarse sugar
Garnish: whipped topping, Caramel Sauce
    (recipe on page 197)

1. Preheat oven to 350°. Line a rimmed baking sheet with parchment paper; set aside.

2. In a large bowl, combine apples, lemon juice, and vanilla.

3. In a small bowl, whisk together sugar, flour, cornstarch, cinnamon, nutmeg, and salt. Add sugar mixture to apples, tossing to coat each slice.

4. On a lightly floured surface, unroll half of dough. Using a pastry brush, lightly coat with water. Place remaining dough on top, pressing to adhere. Roll dough to a ⅛-inch thickness. Cut 6 (6-inch) rounds from dough. Place rounds on prepared pan. Spread each dough round with approximately 1 to 1½ tablespoons Pecan Frangipane, leaving a 2-inch border.

5. Strain apples. Arrange apples onto filling, leaving a 2-inch border. Wrap remaining dough around apples in an overlapping fashion.

6. In a small bowl, whisk together egg and water. Using a pastry brush, lightly coat each galette with egg wash. Sprinkle each with coarse sugar.

7. Bake for about 25 to 30 minutes or until golden brown. Remove from oven, and let cool slightly. Serve warm with whipped topping and Caramel Sauce, if desired. Cover, and refrigerate for up to 3 days.

PECAN FRANGIPANE
Makes 1 cup

1 cup sugar
1 cup pecan halves
1 cup butter, softened
2 large eggs
1 teaspoon vanilla extract
¼ teaspoon salt

1. In the work bowl of a food processor, pulse together sugar and pecans until finely ground. Add butter, and pulse to combine. Add eggs, one at a time, pulsing well after each addition. Add vanilla and salt, and continue to pulse until smooth. Cover, and refrigerate for 1 hour.

Apple Galettes
Makes 6 servings

1¼ pounds Granny Smith apples (about 3 to 4 apples) peeled, cored, and sliced ¼ inch thick
1 tablespoon fresh lemon juice
1 tablespoon vanilla extract
¾ cup sugar, divided
2 tablespoons all-purpose flour
1 tablespoon cornstarch
½ teaspoon ground cinnamon
¼ teaspoon ground nutmeg
⅛ teaspoon salt
1 (14.1-ounce) package refrigerated piecrusts

Cran-Apple Crisp

Makes 1 (13x9-inch) dish

- 8 cups peeled, sliced Pink Lady apples (about 6 apples)
- 2 cups fresh or frozen cranberries
- 1 cup granulated sugar
- 2 tablespoons cornstarch
- ¼ teaspoon ground cinnamon
- ½ teaspoon fresh orange zest
- 2 tablespoons fresh orange juice
- ½ cup unsalted butter, softened
- ⅔ cup firmly packed light brown sugar
- 1 cup all-purpose flour
- ½ cup old-fashioned oats
- ¼ cup chopped pecans
- ¾ teaspoon kosher salt
- Garnish: Caramel Sauce

1. Preheat oven to 350°.

2. In a large bowl, stir together apples, cranberries, granulated sugar, cornstarch, cinnamon, orange zest, and orange juice until combined. Spoon apple mixture into a 13x9-inch baking dish. Set aside.

3. In a large bowl, beat butter and brown sugar with a mixer at medium speed for 3 to 4 minutes or until creamed. Slowly add flour, oats, pecans, and salt until well combined. Crumble butter mixture over apple mixture.

4. Bake until filling is bubbling and top is golden brown, about 1 hour. Cover loosely with foil to prevent excess browning. Drizzle with Caramel Sauce, if desired.

CARAMEL SAUCE

Makes 1½ cups

- 1 cup sugar
- ¼ cup water
- 4 tablespoons unsalted butter, softened
- ½ cup heavy whipping cream, room temperature
- ½ teaspoon kosher salt

1. In a medium saucepan, combine sugar and water. Bring to a boil over medium heat. Cook, without stirring, until mixture is amber in color. Brush sides of pot with water to prevent crystallization.

2. Remove from heat, and stir in butter, cream, and salt. Mixture will boil vigorously. Set aside, and let cool to room temperature.

Pumpkin-Streusel Pie Bars

Makes about 16 bars

- 1¾ cups all-purpose flour
- ⅔ cup quick-cooking oats
- ⅔ cup firmly packed light brown sugar
- 1 teaspoon salt, divided
- 1 cup cold butter, diced
- 1 (16-ounce) can pumpkin
- 1 (14-ounce) can sweetened condensed milk
- 1½ teaspoons pumpkin pie spice
- 1 teaspoon lemon zest
- 2 large eggs

1. Preheat oven to 350°. Line a 9-inch square baking pan with foil, allowing edges to extend over sides of pan. Spray with baking spray with flour.

2. In a large bowl, combine flour, oats, brown sugar, and ½ teaspoon salt. Using a pastry cutter, cut in butter until mixture appears crumbly. Remove 1 cup oat mixture; set aside. Pat remaining oat mixture into the bottom of prepared pan. Bake for 10 minutes. Let cool on a wire rack for 30 minutes.

3. In a large bowl, whisk together pumpkin, condensed milk, pumpkin pie spice, lemon zest, eggs, and remaining ½ teaspoon salt. Pour over cooled crust. Sprinkle with reserved 1 cup oat mixture. Bake until oat mixture is golden brown and filling is set, about 45 minutes. Let cool completely on a wire rack. Refrigerate until chilled, about 4 hours. Using edges of foil, lift from pan. Cut into bars using a serrated knife.

1. Preheat oven to 350°. Spray a 10-inch Bundt pan with baking spray with flour.

2. In a small bowl, combine cranberries and boiling water; let stand for 10 minutes. Drain.

3. In a medium bowl, whisk together flour and pumpkin pie spice.

4. In a large bowl, beat butter, cream cheese, and brown sugar with a mixer at medium speed until creamy. Add eggs, one at a time, beating well after each addition. Add flour mixture; beat until blended. Beat in cranberries, pumpkin, and vanilla. Spoon batter into prepared pan, smoothing top. Tap twice on counter to release air bubbles. Bake until a wooden pick inserted near center comes out clean, about 45 minutes. Let cool in pan for 15 minutes. Remove from pan. Let cool completely on a wire rack. Garnish with confectioners' sugar, if desired.

Pumpkin Scones with Maple-Ginger Glaze

Makes 8 servings

2¼   cups self-rising flour
½   cup firmly packed dark brown sugar
1½   teaspoons pumpkin pie spice
½   cup cold butter, diced
⅔   cup canned pumpkin
3   tablespoons whole milk
1   large egg
  Maple-Ginger Glaze (recipe follows)
⅓   cup chopped toasted pecans
  Garnish: finely chopped crystallized ginger

1. Preheat oven to 375°.

2. In a large bowl, combine flour, brown sugar, and pumpkin pie spice. Using a pastry cutter, cut in butter until mixture appears crumbly.

3. In a small bowl, whisk together pumpkin, milk, and egg. Add pumpkin mixture to flour mixture, stirring until mixture forms a soft, sticky dough. Turn dough out onto a floured surface. Knead gently 3 to 4 times.

Pumpkin-Cranberry Bundt Cake

Makes 8 to 10 servings

¾   cup dried cranberries, chopped
½   cup boiling water
2¾   cups self-rising flour
1½   teaspoons pumpkin pie spice
½   cup unsalted butter, softened
½   (8-ounce) package cream cheese, softened
1¾   cups firmly packed light brown sugar
3   large eggs
1   cup canned pumpkin
2   teaspoons vanilla extract
  Garnish: confectioners' sugar

4. Place dough on a baking sheet. Using floured hands, pat dough into an 8-inch circle. Lightly cut top of dough into 8 wedges, being careful not to cut completely through dough.

5. Bake until golden brown and a wooden pick inserted in center comes out clean, about 20 minutes. Let cool completely on a wire rack. Cut into 8 wedges. Drizzle with Maple-Ginger Glaze. Sprinkle with pecans. Garnish with crystallized ginger, if desired.

MAPLE-GINGER GLAZE
Makes about ⅓ cup

1	cup confectioners' sugar
5	teaspoons whole milk
⅛	teaspoon ground ginger
⅛	teaspoon maple extract

1. In a medium bowl, combine confectioners' sugar, milk, ginger, and maple extract. Stir to form a thin glaze. Use immediately.

piecrust, letting ends extend over edges. Add pie weights or dried beans. Bake for 10 minutes. Carefully remove paper and pie weights; bake for 2 to 3 minutes or until bottom of crust is lightly browned. Let crust cool completely in pan.

3. In a medium bowl, combine hot caramel topping and cream cheese. Beat with a mixer at medium speed until well combined. Spread caramel mixture into prepared crust.

4. In a medium bowl, combine peanut butter and cream. Beat with a mixer at medium speed until stiff peaks form. Spread peanut butter mixture on top of caramel mixture. Drizzle with melted chocolate and chopped peanuts, if desired.

We used Smucker's Hot Caramel Topping.

Hazelnut Brownies
Makes 2 dozen

1 cup butter
5 (1-ounce) squares unsweetened chocolate, chopped
2 cups sugar
5 large eggs
2 cups all-purpose flour
½ teaspoon salt
1 teaspoon vanilla extract
1 (13-ounce) jar chocolate-hazelnut spread*
2 cups semisweet chocolate morsels
½ cup chopped hazelnuts

1. Preheat oven to 350°. Line a 13x9-inch baking pan with heavy-duty foil.

2. In a small microwave-safe bowl, melt butter and chocolate in microwave oven on high in 30-second intervals, stirring between each, until melted (about 1½ minutes total).

3. In a large bowl, combine chocolate mixture and sugar. Beat with a mixer at medium speed until well blended. Add eggs, one at a time, beating well after each addition. Add flour, salt, and vanilla, beating until just combined. Add chocolate-hazelnut spread and chocolate morsels, beating to combine. Spread batter into prepared pan. Sprinkle top of batter with hazelnuts. Bake for 30 to 40 minutes or until a wooden pick inserted in center comes out still slightly sticky. Let cool completely in pan on wire rack.

We used Nutella.

Peanut Butter Tart
Makes 1 (11-inch) tart

1 (14.1-ounce) package refrigerated piecrusts
1 (12-ounce) container hot caramel topping*
1 (8-ounce) package cream cheese, softened
1 cup creamy peanut butter
½ cup heavy whipping cream
Garnish: melted chocolate, chopped honey roasted peanuts

1. Preheat oven to 450°.

2. On a lightly floured surface, place one piecrust on top of second piecrust. Roll crust to a 14-inch circle. Fit piecrust into an 11-inch tart pan with removable bottom. Trim crust to make even with top of tart pan. Place a piece of parchment paper in bottom of

2. In a large bowl, combine butter, brown sugar, and granulated sugar. Beat with a mixer at medium speed until fluffy. Add vanilla, beating to combine. Add eggs, one at a time, beating well after each addition.

3. In a separate bowl, combine flour, baking powder, baking soda, and salt. Gradually add flour mixture to butter mixture, beating at low speed until blended. Stir in butterscotch morsels and toffee bits. Spread batter evenly in pan. Bake for 30 to 40 minutes or until a wooden pick inserted in center comes out clean. Let cool completely in pan on a wire rack.

Pecan Date Pie
Makes 1 (9-inch) deep-dish pie

- ½ (14.1-ounce) package refrigerated piecrusts
- ½ cup firmly packed light brown sugar
- ½ cup light corn syrup
- ½ cup cane syrup
- ¼ cup unsalted butter, melted
- 3 large eggs
- 1½ teaspoons vanilla extract
- ½ teaspoon salt
- 2½ cups pecan halves
- 1 cup chopped and pitted dates
- Garnish: whipped topping, chopped pecans, ground cinnamon

1. Preheat oven to 350°.

2. On a lightly floured surface, roll piecrust to a 12-inch circle. Fit pie crust into a 9-inch deep-dish pie plate. Trim excess dough ½ inch beyond edge of pie plate. Fold edges under, and crimp. Line crust with parchment paper, allowing excess to hang over sides. Add pie weights. Bake for 10 minutes; let cool completely. Remove pie weights, and set aside.

3. In a large bowl, combine brown sugar, corn syrup, and cane syrup. Whisk in melted butter and eggs until well combined. Whisk in vanilla and salt. Sprinkle pecans and dates into bottom of piecrust. Pour brown sugar mixture on top of pecans and dates. Bake for 45 minutes to 1 hour or until center is set. If necessary, cover loosely with foil for the last 20 to 30 minutes of baking to prevent excess browning. Let cool completely on a wire rack before serving. Garnish with whipped topping, chopped pecans, and ground cinnamon, if desired.

Butterscotch Toffee Blondies
Makes about 2 dozen

- 1 cup butter, softened
- 1 cup firmly packed light brown sugar
- ½ cup granulated sugar
- 1 teaspoon vanilla extract
- 3 large eggs
- 3 cups all-purpose flour
- 1½ teaspoons baking powder
- ½ teaspoon baking soda
- ½ teaspoon salt
- 1 (11-ounce) package butterscotch morsels
- 1 (8-ounce) package toffee bits

1. Preheat oven to 350°. Line a 13x9-inch baking pan with foil. Spray foil with baking spray with flour.

ACKNOWLEDGMENTS

Over the years, we have been blessed by the generosity and hospitality of many homeowners, as well as by our friends at some of the finest stores and companies in the world. To them, we offer our sincerest gratitude for their help with the contents of this special volume of collected recipes.

Accents of The South
Anna Weatherley
Annieglass
Anthropologie
At Home Furnishings
Beverly Ruff Antiques and Linens
Billy Cotton
Bungalow Classic
Bromberg's
Canvas
Calico Corners
Dash & Albert
Deborah Rhodes
Dinnerware Depot
Edgar's Bakery
French Laundry Home
Gien
Hen House Linens
Hobby Lobby
HomeGoods
Impulse Enterprise
Juliska
Kim Seybert

The Lamp Shop
Layla Grace
Levy's Fine Jewelry
Le Jacquard Francais
L'Object
Lowe's
Macy's
Mariposa
Michael Aram
Michaels
Mottahedeh
Mulberry Heights Antiques
The Nest
The Optima Company
Pickard
Pier 1 Imports
Pottery Barn
Replacements, LTD.
Rosegate Design
Rosanna
Royal Crown Derby
Shiraleah
Sul La Table
Sweet Peas Garden Shop

Table Matters
Target
Tricia's Treasures
Vagabond House
Vietri
Waterford
West Elm
Whole Foods
Williams-Sonoma
Wisteria
World Market

RECIPE INDEX